Computational Intelligence, Evolutionary Computing and Evolutionary Clustering Algorithms

Authored By

Terje Kristensen
CEO and Founder of Pattern Solutions ltd.
and
Bergen University College
Bergen
Norway

Computational Intelligence, Evolutionary Computing and Evolutionary Clustering Algorithms

Algorithms

Author: Terje Kristensen

ISBN (eBook): 978-1-68108-299-8

ISBN (Print): 978-1-68108-300-1 © 2016, Bentham eBooks imprint.

Published by Bentham Science Publishers – Sharjah, UAE. All Rights Reserved.

First published in 2016.

advertisements or ideas contained in the Work.

Limitation of Liability:

In no event will Bentham Science Publishers, its staff, editors and/or authors, be liable for any damages, including, without limitation, special, incidental and/or consequential damages and/or damages for lost data and/or profits arising out of (whether directly or indirectly) the use or inability to use the Work. The entire liability of Bentham Science Publishers shall be limited to the amount actually paid by you for the Work.

General:

1. Any dispute or claim arising out of or in connection with this License Agreement or the Work (including non-contractual disputes or claims) will be governed by and construed in accordance with the laws of the U.A.E. as applied in the Emirate of Dubai. Each party agrees that the courts of the Emirate of Dubai shall have exclusive jurisdiction to settle any dispute or claim arising out of or in connection with this License Agreement or the Work (including non-contractual disputes or claims).
2. Your rights under this License Agreement will automatically terminate without notice and without the need for a court order if at any point you breach any terms of this License Agreement. In no event will any delay or failure by Bentham Science Publishers in enforcing your compliance with this License Agreement constitute a waiver of any of its rights.
3. You acknowledge that you have read this License Agreement, and agree to be bound by its terms and conditions. To the extent that any other terms and conditions presented on any website of Bentham Science Publishers conflict with, or are inconsistent with, the terms and conditions set out in this License Agreement, you acknowledge that the terms and conditions set out in this License Agreement shall prevail.

Bentham Science Publishers Ltd.
Executive Suite Y - 2
PO Box 7917, Saif Zone
Sharjah, U.A.E.
Email: subscriptions@benthamscience.org

**BENTHAM
SCIENCE**

CONTENTS

"In memory of my mother, Anna, for teaching me never to give up."

PREFACE

This book is about how to use new algorithm models to solve complex problems. The book presents one branch of a field in computer science that we today call computational intelligence. Big Data play already a great role in society and evolutionary algorithms may be one approach to do data mining of high-dimensional data. High-dimensional data are produced in scientific laboratories all over the world and are often difficult to interpret. Clustering is one possible technique that may help us to interpret these data.

Clustering is a well-known technique that is used in many areas of science. This book is about how to use such algorithms to solve clustering of huge sets of data. This subject may be introduced in the last year at the bachelor level in computer science or mathematics or at the graduate level. The intention of the book is to show how to use such computation models on classical clustering problems. Visualization is an important part of the clustering process. We therefore also want to visualize the result of the cluster analysis.

The most known clustering algorithm is the K-means algorithm that is dependent on the parameter value K and the initial position of K cluster centroids. An incorrect value will result in an inaccurate clustering structure. The configuration of cluster centroids determines if the algorithm converges to a local minimum or not. These limitations may be solved by using evolutionary algorithms.

Genetic algorithms and differential evolution algorithms are two paradigms in the book that are used to optimize the value of K and the initial configuration of cluster centroids. The correctness and quality of the solution are compared using both artificial and real-life data sets. Experiments have shown that the algorithms are able to classify the correct number of well-defined clusters, but fail to do so for overlapping data clusters. This is mainly because the Davies-Bouldin Index as a fitness measure has certain kind of limitations. The experiments carried out in the book also show that both Genetic and Differential evolution algorithms provide suboptimal positions of initial configuration of cluster centroids, reflected in higher values of the Davies-Bouldin Index.

ACKNOWLEDGEMENTS

I will thank Bergen University College for making it possible to write this book. I also thank Bentham Science Publishers for all help and specifically Manager for Publications, Salma Sarfaraz, for all the support during the publishing process. At last I will thank my prior master student Eirik Steine Frivåg who has contributed a lot in this book.

CONFLICT OF INTEREST

The author confirms that there is no conflict of interest to declare for this publication.

Terje Kristensen
Bergen University College
Bergen
Norway
E-mail: tkr@hib.no

CHAPTER 1

Introduction

Abstract: This chapter describes the main goal of the book, namely the use of evolutionary algorithms to optimize the K-means algorithm. The outline of the book is also given in the chapter.

Keywords: Background, Case study, Data visualization, Design and implementation, Discussion, Evolutionary algorithms, Introduction, System specification, User interface.

1.1. OVERVIEW

The *K-means algorithm* is one of the most applied algorithms of partitional clustering, where it aims to partition n data objects into K clusters (or groups) based on some dissimilarity measure. The number of clusters K is predefined. A major drawback of the algorithm is that its performance is dependent on the pre-defined value of K, because it produces a clustering structure under the assumption that the number of clusters in the data is K. If the predefined K is not accurate, the algorithm converge into a local minimum. This means that there exists a better solution to the clustering problem. Much can be gained in terms of performance by providing the optimal value of K. The purpose of clustering is to analyse unknown data, thus making the task of predefining a good value of K an impossible task. Various *Optimization* techniques have been applied to find the best value of K for a given clustering problem. Evolutionary algorithms are heuristic optimization algorithms that mimic the process of *natural selection* from biology. They have gained a lot of interest because of its abilities to find global optimal solutions to an optimization problem. *Genetic algorithms* define a para-digm within evolutionary algorithms that model genetic evolution by evolving a population of candidate solutions, to find the optimal solution of a problem. There has been extensive research on adapting genetic algorithms to K-means algorithm, with varying results.

Differential Evolution is another paradigm of evolutionary algorithms that focus on using information about the current population to perform a more intelligent search for an optimal solution. By utilizing information about the search space, we may guide the candidate solutions into more promising areas of the search space, which may produce a better result and also possible increase the convergence speed of the algorithm.

1.2. GOAL

The main goal of this project (book) is to explore the possibilities of adapting evolutionary algorithms to optimize the K-means algorithm. The purpose is to create an evolutionary clustering algorithm that locates the value of *K*, with corresponding cluster centroids, that produces an optimal clustering structure of a given data set. As a part of the research we may adapt both a *Genetic algorithm* and a *Differential Evolution* algorithm to the K-means algorithm, to compare their performance using benchmark tests. As a result, a system is created that performs cluster analysis using evolutionary clustering algorithms. *Visualization* is an important part of clustering to be able to visualize the result of the cluster analysis graphically. Analysing high-dimensional data impose restrictions on how we may visualize the data. We therefore need to present the data in a way that comply to these restrictions.

1.3. OUTLINE

Chapter 1 (Introduction)

This chapter gives a brief overview of the problem domain and presents the goals of this project.

Chapter 2 (Background)

This chapter presents relevant background theory of the main subjects of the book. The chapter is divided into two parts. The first part provides a detailed introduction to the field of cluster analysis, where we focus on presenting the main concepts of cluster analysis. The second part gives an introduction to mathematical optimization.

Chapter 3 (Evolutionary Algorithms)

This chapter gives an introduction to evolutionary algorithms, including an introduction to different paradigms of evolutionary algorithms.

Chapter 4 (System Specification)

This chapter presents the main objectives of the system developed, including both the functional and the non-functional requirements.

Chapter 5 (Design and Implementation)

This chapter provides a description of the overall design of the system and algorithms. First, we describe the overall architecture, including different design patterns applied for the implementation. Second, we will describe the design of relevant algorithms along with the time complexity of them.

Chapter 6 (Data Visualization)

We introduce here the subject of visualization and its application within the system.

Chapter 7 (User Interface)

In this chapter, we describe the user interface of the system.

Chapter 8 (Case Study)

Some cases are studied to compare different clustering algorithms using both artificial and real-life data sets.

Chapter 9 (Discussion)

In this chapter we discuss different aspects and design challenges of adapting evolutionary algorithms to optimize the K-means algorithm.

Chapter 10 (Summary and Future Directions)

The chapter gives a summary of the project and the work performed to achieve the goals. This includes suggestions on how to improve the system and some ideas for future work.

Computational Intelligence, 2016, 7-23

CHAPTER 2

Background

Abstract: The chapter describes three phases of a pattern recognition system; data acquisition, feature extraction and classification. In addition, different clustering methods are described.

Keywords: Cluster validation, Fuzzy clustering, Hierarchical methods, Partitional clustering.

2.1. CLUSTERING

2.1.1. Introduction

The amount of information available on the Internet is enormous, but only a fraction is relevant to each user. People may only dedicate much time in their busy schedule to consume information, if it is important and only the most valuable information should be presented. As a result, we need information filtering systems. A good example is an e-mail inbox. Without an automatic spam filter, users have to spend their time going through irrelevant email, containing malware, advertisement and other unwanted content. The purpose of an automatic spam filter is to remove unwanted e-mail before it reach the inbox so that only relevant information is presented to the user. A spam filter consists of different criteria, or rules, that are used to filter out spam e-mail. Some of the criteria are generally based on what the general public defines as spam. For instance, e-mail containing the phrase *"Money Back Guarantee"* is in most cases spam [1]. Other criteria are based on a training set generated through interaction with the user. The training set consists of e-mail that is manually identified as *"wanted"* and *"unwanted"*. The filter uses this set as a template for future classification [2].

Over time the training set will evolve, thus making the classification more accurate.

The example above describes a pattern recognition system. A pattern recognition system consists of three phases; *Data acquisition, Feature extraction* and *Classification* [3]. In the data acquisition phase the system gathers data by using some set of sensors depending on the environment of the data, to be acquired. In the example above the gathered data would be incoming emails. The system then extracts the features of the data. The purpose of this phase is to select a set of features to be used to classify the data. There are two critical aspects of this phase [3]:

1. One has to choose a criterion for evaluating the significance of a feature.
2. One needs to find the optimal size of the feature set.

In the classification phase the extracted data points are mapped into a set of classes or groups. To summarize, pattern recognition is a transformation from the measurement space M, containing the acquired data, to the feature space F and to the classification space D [3], *i.e.*

$$M \rightarrow F \rightarrow D. \tag{2.1}$$

The spam filter classification process is an example of *supervised classification*. Supervised classification is possible when you have a priori information about the dataset, where there is already established a model of the problem domain [4]. There already exist labelled data, meaning that some patterns are already classified, and this labelled data could be used as a training set to generate the classification criteria. The actual training is done based on a classifier function, D. Given a N-dimensional input pattern $\mathbf{x} = [x_1, x_2,...,x_N]$ the function $D(x)$ will classify the pattern as member of one of k possible classes, $C_1, C_2, ..., C_k$. The training process consists of optimizing the parameters of D to best fit the training set [3], where one adjusts the parameters so that the classifier function is able to map each input pattern to the corresponding class of the training set. After optimizing the parameters of D, the system should be able to classify an unknown pattern into the correct class. The error rate depends on the maturity of the training set where more diversity in the training examples will give a more well-defined classifier function. More details on optimization will be discussed later in the book.

But how do you find patterns and hidden structures in unlabelled data? In biology this process is called *Taxonomy*. In the field of data mining this is known as *unsupervised classification, clustering* or *cluster analysis*. The outline of Section 2.1 is as follows: Section 2.1.2 will describe the general definition of clustering. In 2.1.3 one covers definition of similarity between objects. In 2.1.4 we give an introduction to the various clustering methods, and 2.1.5 covers *crisp* and *fuzzy* clustering. At last in 2.1.6 we present *cluster validation*, how to validate the result of the cluster analysis.

2.1.2. General Definition

In biology, *Taxonomy* is known as the science of identifying and naming unknown species and organizing them into a system [5]. The purpose is to organize species in groups based on some common characteristics. The same idea is brought into data mining, especially in clustering where the objective is the same, namely organizing and grouping data objects into different clusters based on common characteristic. There exist various definitions of a cluster, depending on the clustering method. Hierarchical methods, see section 2.1.4, organize clusters based on the distance between objects, and partitional methods creating clusters based on minimization of the mean square error of the clusters. However, what all definitions have in common are that they describe an internal homogeneity and an external separation [6]. This means that, based on some measure of similarity, an object is similar to other objects within the same cluster and dissimilar to objects that are not in the same cluster. The various clustering methods, including the previous two, will be discussed in section 2.1.4 of the book. The general mathematical definition is that you have a set S of n patterns, $S = \{x_1, x_2,...,x_N\}$ where each pattern is denoted as a vector in a N-dimensional feature space, $x = [x_1, x_2, \ldots, x_j, \ldots, x_N]$ [3]. These patterns are partitioned into K clusters, $C_1, C_2, ..., C_K$, where

$$C_i \neq \emptyset, \qquad \text{for i} = 1, \ldots, K, \qquad\qquad \textbf{(2.2a)}$$

$$C_i \cap C_j = \varnothing, \qquad \text{for } i = 1, \ldots, K,\ j = 1, \ldots, K, \text{and } i \neq j, \text{ and} \qquad \textbf{(2.2b)}$$

$$\bigcup_{i=1}^{K} C_i = S. \qquad \textbf{(2.2c)}$$

The result of the cluster analysis is usually represented as a partition $U(x)$ where $U = u_{kj}$, $k = 1, \ldots, K$ and $j = 1, \ldots, n$, representing the membership of pattern x_j to cluster C_k.

2.1.3. Object Similarity

The definition of similarity is highly dependent on the characteristics of the data analysed. Through feature extraction and selection the most significant features are selected. How each feature is represented is an important factor when comparing the objects. A pattern is represented as a multi-dimensional vector where each dimension represents a specific feature.

Features may be classified as *continuous* or *discrete* [6]. Continuous features are features that are uncountable and can have any value within some range (infinity), *e.g.* the height of a person can have any value larger than 0. Discrete features on the other hand can only have some specific values, *e.g.* the number of students in a class must be an integer value because you can't have a half student in a class. A subcategory of discrete features is *binary* features, which can only have two values, **1** or **0**. Another property of a feature is the *measurement level*. A feature is usually represented by numbers. The measurement level describes how these numbers can be used [6]. The scale may consist of four levels, from lowest to highest:

1. *Nominal.* A nominal feature is represented by explicit labels or names, *i.e.* gender. These features have no mathematical significance.
2. *Ordinal.* As with nominal feature ordinal features are represented by labels. The difference between the values are meaningless, but there is a certain order implied, *i.e.* "small", "medium" and "large".
3. *Internal.* For these features the difference between the values makes sense, but there exists no meaningful ratio between them because it does not exist any

absolute zero value. An example is the temperature measurement unit Celsius. 200°C is hotter than 100°C, but cooking a cake for 30 minutes at 200°C will not yield the same result as cooking it for one hour at 100°C. 200°C is not twice as hot as 100°C because of a non-existent absolute zero value.

4. *Ratio.* The ratio feature possesses all the previous features, but in addition there exists an absolute zero value. This means that there also exists a meaningful interpretation of the ratio between two values. For instance, 50 $ is twice as much as 25 $ because of the absolute zero value of 0 $.

Proximity measures are used to define similarity or dissimilarity between objects in some metric space [6].

A metric space is a set *M* with a corresponding dissimilarity function *D* that measures the distance between the elements of *M* [7]. *D* is also known as a *metric*. A dissimilarity function *D* has to satisfy these requirements:

1. *Symmetry,*

$$D(x_i, x_j) = D(x_j, x_i)$$

$$\text{(2.3a)}$$

2. *Positivity,*

$$\forall x_i, \forall x_j : D(x_i, x_j) \geq 0$$

$$\text{(2.3b)}$$

3. *Triangle inequality*

$$\forall x_i, \forall x_j, \forall x_k : D(x_i, x_j) \leq D(x_i, x_k) + D(x_k, x_j)$$

$$\text{(2.3c)}$$

4. *Reflexivity*

$$D(x_i, x_j) = 0 \iff x_i = x_j$$

$$\text{(2.3d)}$$

Given these requirements a dissimilarity function will produce an output where $D(x_i, x_j) \geq D(x_i, x_k)$ if x_i and x_j is more dissimilar (or non-equal) than x_i and x_k. A similarity function, also known as a *similarity metric*, *S* have to satisfy these requirements [6]:

1. *Symmetry,*

$$S(x_i, x_j) = S(x_j, x_i) \tag{2.4a}$$

2. *Positivity,*

$$\forall x_i, \forall x_j : 0 \leq S(x_i, x_j) \leq 1 \tag{2.4b}$$

3. *Triangle inequality*

$$S(x_i, x_j)S(x_j, x_k) \leq [S(x_i, x_j) + S(x_j, x_k)]S(x_i, x_k) \tag{2.4c}$$

4. *Reflexivity*

$$S(x_i, x_j) = 1 \iff x_i = x_j \tag{2.4d}$$

Usage of similarity or dissimilarity measure depends on the previously feature properties in the last paragraph. For a data set of N objects, we can represent similarity/dissimilarity measure between objects in a $N \times N$ proximity matrix P. $P[i,j]$ represents the dissimilarity measure between objects i, j.

Proximity Measure for Continuous Values

For continuous values it is most common to use distance functions (dissimilarity) as proximity measure [6]. An example is the *Euclidean distance* between two vectors, x_i and x_j, represented as,

$$D(x_i, x_j) = \sqrt{\sum_{l=1}^{d}(x_{il} - x_{jl})^2} \tag{2.5}$$

where d represents the vector dimension. A problem with this function is that each feature can be measured in different units, which means that units with large variance may dominate. A common solution to this problem is to *normalize* the data objects so that each feature contributes equally. A proposed normalization method is *min-max normalization* that focuses on the minimum and maximum values of each feature, transforming values of each feature into the range of [0, 1] [8] . Given the minimum value, *minl*, and maximum value, *maxl*, of the *l*th feature of vector x_i, the normalized feature value, denoted as x′*il*, is produced by

$$x'_{il} = \frac{x_{il} - min_l}{max_l - min_l}$$

(2.6)

where x_{il} is the original value of the *l*th feature.

Proximity Measure for Discrete Values

The similarity between features represented by discrete values tend to be high because the number of different values is smaller than continuous values [6]. Because of this, it is more common to use similarity functions as proximity measures. Discrete binary values could be used to represent gender, where each value is equally important, *i.e.* 0 represents *male* and 1 represents *female*. This is called a symmetric feature. Asymmetric features are features where one value is more significant than the other. One example of this is when the binary value represents the existence/absence of a feature. Absent features is less valuable than existing features.

Proximity Measure for Mixed Values

It is common that object features are represented by a mix of both continuous and discrete values, resulting in problems when comparing objects. To overcome these obstacles one could map the values from one value type to the other, but this also has its shortcomings. One could map all discrete values into an interval of [0, 1], but this is not possible when some features are represented by label values with no mathematical significance. One could also transform continuous values into discrete values, but then one would most likely suffer from information loss. In [6] one describes a more powerful method where the proximity measure uses a combination of similarity and distance functions to compare objects. The similarity measure between objects x_i and x_j containing mixed feature values is defined as

$$S(x_i, x_j) = \frac{\sum_{l=1}^{d} \delta_{ijl} S_{ijl}}{\sum_{l=1}^{d} \delta_{ijl}} \tag{2.7}$$

where d denotes the vector dimension. δ_{ijl} is a 0-1 coefficient that takes care of missing feature measures. Data sets are not always perfect and data objects with missing feature values should not be considered when calculating proximity. The coefficient is defined as

$$\delta_{ijl} = \begin{cases} 1, & \text{if } x_{il} \text{ or } x_{jl} \text{ is missing} \\ 0, & \text{otherwise.} \end{cases} \tag{2.8}$$

S_{ijl} represents the similarity measure between object i and j. For discrete values, S_{ijl} is given as

$$S_{ijl} = \begin{cases} 1, & \text{if } x_{il} = x_{jl} \\ 0, & \text{if } x_{il} \neq x_{jl} \end{cases} \tag{2.9}$$

and for continuous values it is given as

$$S_{ijl} = 1 - \frac{|x_{il} - x_{jl}|}{R_l} \tag{2.10}$$

where R_l is the range of the lth feature.

2.1.4. Clustering Methods

Hierarchical Clustering

The purpose of *Hierarchical clustering* is to build a hierarchy of clusters. There are two general approaches to this method, namely *Agglomerative* and *Divisive* [6]. The *agglomerative* approach is a bottom-up strategy where you start off with all data objects as individual clusters. You then need to find the two clusters that are closest together by some distance measure and merge them into the same cluster [7]. This merging process continues until you have one big super cluster containing all data points. The result usually illustrated in a *Dendogram*, a tree diagram, showing how close the data objects are to each other. The root of the tree represents the whole data set, while leaf nodes represents data objects. The height h of the tree represents the relationship between clusters, illustrated in Fig. (**2.1**). Given a pair of data points, x_i and x_j, h_{ij} represent the height of the smallest subtree of which both data points are member. A small value of h_{ij} indicates that the data points are close together. In Fig. (**2.1**) the internal node representing the smallest subtree that both x_1 and x_2 belong to, has a lower h-value than the internal node representing the smallest sub-tree where both x_1 and x_4 belong, meaning that x_1 and x_2 are more similar than x_1 and x_4.

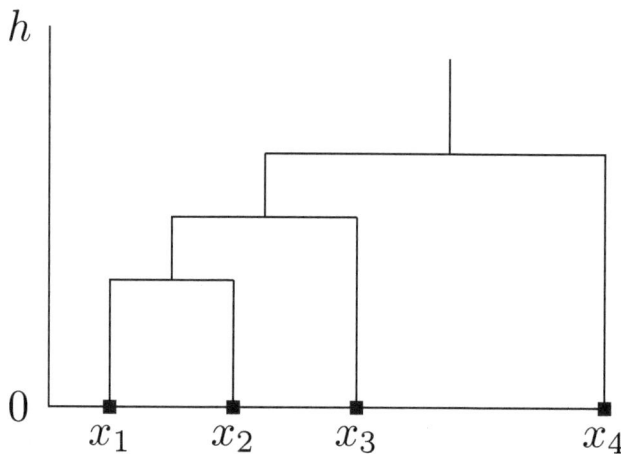

Fig. (2.1). Dendogram.

The simplest agglomerative method is the *Single-link method*. This method uses nearest neighbour as a dissimilarity measure, meaning that the two closest data points in some N-dimensional space are the two data points with the smallest Euclidean distance (see Equation 2.5) . The clusters with the smallest Euclidean distance will be merged together in the merging process. In contrast to the agglomerative approach, the D*ivisive* method is a *top-down* strategy where you start with all data points belonging to a single cluster and divide the cluster in half according to some division criteria until each data point makes up their own cluster as the only member [7]. The number of clusters increases by one at each stage of the algorithm. The problem with this approach is choosing the optimal point of division, because given a cluster there are $2^{|C|-1}$ -1 (|C| = cardinality of C) different ways to divide the cluster in two. None of the two approaches will give an optimal partitioning of the clusters, both just produce a hierarchy structure of the data.

The user have to decide the appropriate partitioning by choosing where to cut the clustering hierarchy, *e.g.* choosing the appropriate height h in the dendrogram of Fig. (**2.1**).

Partitional Clustering

Partitional clustering organizes objects into a predefined number of crisp clusters based on some similarity or distance measure. These algorithms are also known as *center-based algorithms* [7]. There usually exists some objective function, used to evaluate how good the clustering result is, making the purpose of the algorithm to evolve the cluster partitioning to minimize the objective function. An example of a partitional clustering algorithm is the *K-means* algorithm, where the objective is to minimize the objective function defined as

$$J = \sum_{j=1}^{n} \sum_{k=1}^{K} u_{kj} \, || \, x_j - z_k \, ||^2 \qquad\qquad (2.11)$$

where u_{kj} is 1 if the *j*th pattern belongs to cluster k, otherwise 0. x_j represents the *j*th pattern and z_k is the "center" of cluster k, also known as the *centroid*. The objective function will be minimized when the distance between the center and the members of a cluster is the smallest (for all *K*-clusters). The algorithm consists of an *initialization* step and an *iteration* step. The initialization step one randomly selects K patterns from the data set to represent the center of each cluster, also known as the *mean*. In the iteration step one computes the Euclidean distance, defined in equation 2.5, between each pattern and each cluster, and assigns a pattern to a cluster based on the smallest distance. Finally, each mean $z_1^{*}, z_2^{*}, \ldots,$ z_k^{*} is updated based on the new members of the each cluster, creating a new "center" of the cluster. This is done as follows [3]:

$$z_i^* = \frac{1}{n_i} \sum_{x_j \in C_i} x_j, \quad i = 1, 2, \ldots, K. \tag{2.12}$$

where N_i is the number of elements belonging to cluster C_i. The algorithm terminates when all centroids stay constant, $z_i^* = z_i^*$, where $i = 1 \ldots K$. The pseudocode for the K-means algorithm is shown in Algorithm **2.1.1**.

Algorithm 2.1.1 Pseudocode for the K-means algorithm

Choose K data objects randomly from the data set S to represent the cluster centroid, C_i;
while $z_i^* \neq z_i$, where $i = 1 \ldots K$ **do**
    for all $x_j \in S$ **do**
        Assign x_j to the closest cluster C_i, based on some dissimilarity function;
    end for
    for $i \leftarrow 1, K$ **do**
        Update centroid based on equation 2.12
    end for
end while

Fuzzy Clustering

Fuzzy clustering differs from traditional clustering in the sense that a data point may be a member of different clusters at the same time. In traditional or *crisp* clustering methods a data point can only belong to one cluster. Traditional crisp clustering only works well when the data is *well-separated*. This means that the objects of a data set is structured in such a manner that it is easy to classify clusters. An example of the difference between well-separated and not well-separated data is illustrated in Fig. (**2.2**). Classifying clusters in Fig. (**2.2a**) is for any clustering algorithm trivial because the structure of the data presents a clear separation of the different clusters and its members. Fig. (**2.2b**) illustrates data where the number of clusters is not evident. Even when assuming an apriori known number of clusters it would be challenging to divide the data into groups since some data points could have the same distance to different clusters. Thus, the points could be a member of any of these clusters [9]. The idea of fuzzy clustering came from fuzzy set theory where objects have degrees of membership to different sets, in contrast to crisp clustering where an object either is member of a set or not [7]. Given a data point x and the fuzzy set A the membership function $f_A(x)$ determines the degree of membership x has to set A. Values close to 1 indicates higher membership to set A. For a set of data points $X = x$ and two fuzzy set A and B we define the properties for fuzzy sets as:

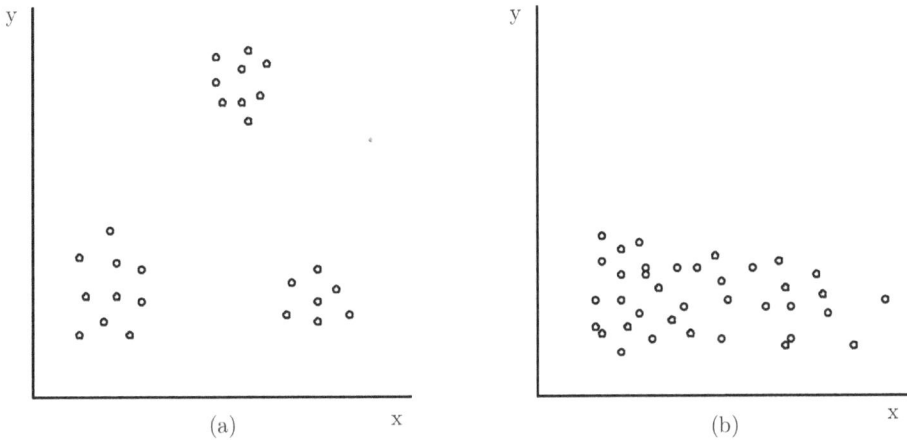

Fig. (2.2). (a) Example of well-separated data and **(b)** Example of data that is not well-separated.

1. *Emptiness.* A fuzzy set is empty if $\forall x : f_A(x) = 0$.
2. *Equal.* Two fuzzy sets, A and B, are equal if their membership functions are equal for all values of x, $A = B \iff \forall x : f_A(x) = f_B(x)$.
3. *Complement.* The complement of the fuzzy set A, A', is defined by

$$\forall x : f_{A'}(x) = 1 - f_A(x)$$

4. *Containment.* A is a subset of B if and only if $\forall x : f_A(x) \leq f_B(x)$
5. *Union.* In regular set theory the union of two sets contain all members of both sets, *e.g.* given set $A = \{1, 2, 3\}$ and $B = \{3, 4, 5\}$ the union of A and B, $A \cup B = \{1, 2, 3, 4, 5\}$. In fuzzy set theory the union of two fuzzy sets are defined as $A \cup B = \max\{f_A(x), f_B(x)\}$. For data point x the union will result in the largest value of the two membership functions.
6. *Intersection.* The intersection between two fuzzy sets, A and B, results in a new fuzzy set containing the minimum value of the two membership functions, that

is $A \cap B = \min\{f_A(x), f_B(x)\}$.

An example of a fuzzy clustering algorithm, an variation of the partitional K-means algorithm, is the *fuzzy c-means* algorithm (FCM). Instead of evolving a cluster partition where each pattern exclusively belongs to one cluster, one evolves a partition where each pattern belongs to every cluster to some degree. As with the K-means algorithm the number of clusters are decided apriori. The objective function is defined as

$$J_\mu(U, Z) = \sum_{i=1}^{c} \sum_{k=1}^{n} (u_{ik})^\mu D^2(z_i, x_k). \tag{2.13}$$

where U is a fuzzy $c \times n$ partition matrix and $u_{ik} \in [0, 1]$ represents the degree of membership for ith pattern of the kth cluster; $\mu \in [1, \infty)$ is a weighting exponent on each fuzzy membership that determines the level of fuzziness on each membership value; Z contains c cluster centers; and is the distance from patterns x_k to center z_k of cluster k. An important property of U is that $\forall k: \sum_{i=1}^{c} u_{ik} = 1$. As with the K-means algorithm, one starts by choosing a number of cluster centers. The fuzzy partition matrix is filled by using the membership value defined beneath [10]

$$u_{ik} = \frac{1}{\sum_{j=1}^{c} \left(\frac{d_{ik}}{d_{jk}}\right)^{\frac{2}{\mu-1}}} \tag{2.14}$$

where d_{ik} is the Euclidean distance between pattern I and center k. We update the center for all clusters as in [10].

$$z_i = \frac{\sum_{k=1}^{n} (u_{ik})^\mu x_k}{\sum_{k=1}^{n} (u_{ik})^\mu}, \quad 1 \le i \le c. \tag{2.15}$$

This is repeated until the change in partition matrix U is less than the termination criterion c, where $c \in [0, 1]$.

2.1.5. Cluster Membership

Cluster membership can be C*risp* or F*uzzy* [3]. The criteria of crisp membership is that a pattern x can only be a member of one of the available clusters A_k. $u_{kj} = 1$ if the pattern x is a member of cluster k, otherwise 0. With fuzzy membership, each pattern can be a member of all k clusters, but in various degree. u_{kj}, where $0 \leq u_{kj} \leq 1$, denotes the degree of membership of the cluster k.

2.1.6. Cluster Validation

Applying different clustering algorithms to a data set or just changing the parameters of an algorithm will result in a different cluster structure [6]. Some clustering structures can also be cluttered and therefore hard to analyse. To compare the various approaches one needs methods for evaluating how meaningful a clustering structure is. This is known as *cluster validation*. With respect to the various clustering methods, outlined in section 2.1.4, there are three measuring criteria [6]:

- *External criteria*
- *Internal criteria*
- *Relative criteria*

Given a data set X and a clustering structure A of X, *external criteria* will compare C to a predefined structure that reflects some apriori information about the clustering structure of X [6]. This criterion can be applied when working with data where there already exists some class labels that can be used for benchmarking. These predefined structures are usually generated by experts, and an external criterion measures how similar the produced clustering structure C is to the predefined structure. These criteria are similar to evaluation methods used for supervised classification described in section 2.1.1. An example of an external criterion is the *Rand index* [6] where the data set X contains a clustering structure of two clusters, A_1 and A_2. We may then define for all data objects $x_i, x_j \in X$ where $x_i \neq x_j$:

- a, as the number of (x_i, x_j)-pairs that belongs to the same cluster in C_1 and C_2,
- b, as the number of (x_i, x_j)-pairs that belongs to different clusters in C_1 and C_2,

- c, as the number of (x_i, x_j)-pairs that belong to the same cluster in C_1 and to different clusters in C_2,
- d, as the number of (x_i, x_j)-pairs that belong to different clusters in C_1 and to the same clusters in C_2.

Based on this, the Rand index is calculated as in [6]

$$R = \frac{(a+d)}{M} \tag{2.16}$$

where M represents the number of possible (x_i, x_j)-pairs, thereby $M = a + b + c + d$. The rand index will result in a number between 0 and 1, where a rand index of 1 means that the clusters are identical and a rand index of 0 means that the clusters are not equal in any way. An *internal criterion* evaluates C exclusively without any a priori information about X. This is done by evaluating the proximity matrix of the clustering structure, defined in section 2.1.3. The *relative criteria* evaluate the clustering structure C of data set X by comparing C to other clustering structures of X produced by other algorithms or different parameters of the same algorithm. An example of a relative criterium is the *Dunn index* [6] which has the purpose of identifying clusters that are compact, and well separated from others. As the name suggests the relative criteria are useful when comparing algorithms. An example is the *K-means algorithm* (see Algorithm **2.1.1**) where the resulting clustering structure of the analysis is dependent on a user defined input K parameter to the algorithm. The relative criteria could be used to evaluate the various resulting clustering structures when different values of K is applied [6]. Given two cluster C_i and C_j, the distance D between them is defined as

$$D(C_i, C_j) = \min_{x \in C_i, y \in C_j} D(x, y), \tag{2.17}$$

i.e. the minimum distance between two points, x and y, where $x \in C_i$ and $y \in C_j$. The diameter of a cluster C_i is defined as

$$diam(C_i) = \max_{x,y \in C_i} D(x, y) \tag{2.18}$$

i.e. the diameter of a cluster is the maximum distance between two members of the cluster. Based on equation 2.17 and 2.18, the Dunn index is defined as

$$Du(K) = \min_{i=1,...,K} \left(\min_{j=i+1,...,K} \left(\frac{D(C_i, C_j)}{\max_{l=1,...,K} diam(C_l)} \right) \right) \tag{2.19}$$

where K is the number of clusters. A compact and well separated clustering structure will result in a large value for the Dunn index. K is then a good estimate of the optimal number of clusters.

A similar validation index is proposed in [11], known as the *Davies-Bouldin Index*. The Index uses intra- and intercluster distances to evaluate the clustering structure of a dataset. As with the Dunn index, validation that yields good results imply a clustering structure that consists of compact and well separated clusters. The index is defined in [12] as

$$DB(K) = \frac{1}{K} \sum_{i=1}^{K} \max_{i \neq j} \left\{ \frac{diam(C_i) + diam(C_j)}{D(C_i, C_j)} \right\} \tag{2.20}$$

where K is the number of clusters, $diam(C_i)$ and $diam(C_j)$ is defined in Equation 2.18 and $D(C_i, C_j)$ is defined in Equation 2.17. A minimized value of $DB(K)$ represents the optimal value of K.

The *Silhouette index* [12] is a validation criteria that measures the average correctness of the clustering structure. Given a cluster C_j (where $j = 1 \ldots K$) with m members, each member is assigned a quality measure known as the *Silhouette width*, denoted by $s(i)$, where $i = 1 \ldots m$. The silhouette width represents how well each member has been clustered. A well clustered object is an object that has been assigned to the most appropriate cluster [12]. The silhouette width is defined as

$$s(i) = \frac{b(i) - a(i)}{\max\{a(i), b(j)\}} \tag{2.21}$$

where $a(i)$ denotes the average distance between the ith member and the rest of the members of C_j. $b(j)$ denotes the minimum average distance from the ith member to all members of cluster C_l, where $l = 1 \ldots K$ and $l \neq j$. A value of $s(i)$ close to 1 imply that data objects i are well clustered [12]. $s(i)$ close to 0 imply that the ith object could be a member of the nearest neighbouring cluster, meaning that the object could be assigned to either cluster indifferently. A value close to -1 illustrates that the object has been misplaced. For a cluster j the average silhouette value S_j is defined in [12] as

$$S_j = \frac{1}{m} \sum_{i=1}^{m} s(i)$$

(2.22)

and thus, for a clustering structure U a global silhouette value is defined as

$$GS_u = \frac{1}{k} \sum_{i=1}^{k} S_j.$$

(2.23)

CHAPTER 3

Evolutionary Algorithms

Abstract: The chapter describes different components of evolutionary algorithms and what is meant by mathematical optimization. In addition, genetic and evolutionary programming is defined.

Keywords: Chromosome, Crossover, Cultural algorithms, Differential evolution, Fitness function, Genetic and evolutionary programming, Mutation, Reproduction, Selection.

3.1. INTRODUCTION

Evolutionary algorithms are based on the principles of evolution and Darwin's theory on "natural selection" [13]. In an environment with limited resources individuals have to compete for survival. All individuals possess various properties (traits) and the individuals that are able to best adapt to the environment, *i.e.* individuals with the superior properties, will survive. As time goes on these individuals will mutate, creating individuals that are more adapted to the environment. This idea is brought into computational intelligence where one solves computer based optimization problems by using evolutionary principles from biology. A generic evolutionary algorithm consists of a population of individuals that all propose a solution to an optimization problem. Each individual has a level of fitness representing the strength of the individual or how good the solution is. *Mutation* and *reproduction* operators are used to evolve the population, where solutions with higher fitness are kept while others are discarded. The algorithm terminates when some stopping condition is fulfilled. In the next paragraphs we will describe all these components in detail.

3.1.1. Data Representation Chromosome

Finding the best solution of a mathematical function consists of optimizing each parameter value to produce an optimal value. This process is known as *mathematical optimization*, described in section 3.2. In an evolutionary algorithm the properties of an individual represent one combination of possible values of these parameters, and hence a possible solution to the optimization problem. Each possible solution is known as a *chromosome* where its parameter values are referred to as *genes* [13]. There exist two types of properties:

- *Genotype*, describes properties of an individual that are represented by genes that may be passed from one generation to the next.
- *Phenotype*, describes behavioural properties.

Genes can be represented by binary, discrete or continuous values. In a standard evolutionary algorithm the size of each chromosome is the same for all individuals of the population.

3.1.2. Initial Population

The first step of the algorithm is to generate the initial population. The initial population consists of individuals where gene values are randomly generated, with the purpose of creating a population where its members are well distributed across the entire search space. Each individual has a unique combination of genes to avoid redundant solutions to the optimization problem. The size of the initial population affects the computational complexity of the algorithm and its ability to explore the entire search space. A large population size will increase diversity and favour exploration, but also increases the computational complexity of each generation.

3.1.3. Fitness Function

The fitness function is a mathematical measure of how good an individual is, where the most fitted individuals are more likely to survive to the next generation. The fitness function *f* maps a chromosome representation into a scalar value

$$f : \Gamma^{n_x} \to \mathbb{R} \tag{3.1}$$

where Γ represents the data type of the elements of a n_x-dimensional chromosome. The formulation of the fitness function is problem dependent, *e.g.* if the parameters are *constrained/unconstrained*, and also if fitness is *absolute* or *relative*. If one has an unconstrained problem one could simply use the objective function as a fitness function, but for constrained problems the parameter constraints need to be included in the function. *Absolute fitness* values are not dependent on fitness of other individuals of the population, while *relative fitness* values are dependent.

3.1.4. Selection

When selecting individuals for reproduction one wants to select individuals with a high fitness level, and thus ensuring a high fitness level of the offspring. This also applies when selecting individuals for the next generation. There are various ways of selecting individuals, where each one is characterized by their *selective pressure*. Selective pressure is a measurement relating to how long it takes for a population to entirely contain the best solution when one only applies the selection operator. High selective pressure will reduce diversity, and thus disfavours exploration. This means that the algorithm converges faster and most likely get stuck in local minima. Too low selective pressure on the other hand results in a slow convergence. Some examples of selection operators are:

- Random Selection
- Proportional Selection
- Tournament Selection
- Rank-based Selection

Different algorithms use different selection operators. A more detailed description of the operators will be given in the chapters describing the different evolutionary algorithms. To ensure that the best individuals survive to the next generation, one could apply elitism where the best individuals are automatically kept for the next generation without being mutated. One could also apply *Hall of fame* where the best individuals in each generation are kept and used as a parent pool for reproduction, ensuring that only the best individuals gets selected for reproduction.

3.1.5. Reproduction

Reproduction is the process of producing a new individual either by combining genetic material from selected individuals or altering genotype of an already existing individual. There are two types of reproduction operators, known as *crossover* and *mutation*. The purpose of applying the crossover operator is to exploit promising areas of the search space, while the mutation operator is applied with the purpose of exploring the total search space. The crossover operator creates an offspring by combining genotypes from two or more individuals. The selection operators, described in the former paragraph, are used to select individuals for crossover. Mutation is the process of randomly altering the genotype of an individual with the purpose of introducing new genetic material to the population and thereby increasing *genetic diversity*. Genetic diversity refers to the degree of variation in the genetic material of individuals in a population, *i.e.* the number of different genotypes that exists in the population. A low degree of genetic diversity indicates a population consisting of individuals that posses the same properties. Reproduction operators are applied with a probability, termed *crossover rate* and *mutation rate*, respectively. One should apply reproduction operators with care since they both affect the convergence time. If the selection operator used for crossover has a high selective pressure one may end up with premature convergence since diversity into the population is disfavored. By applying mutation one brings new genetic material to the population, but one also risks altering individuals with a high fitness level. Because of this, the mutation rate should be quite low. In [13] one recommends that mutation is applied with a high probability in early generations to promote exploration and then decreasing the probability over time to promote exploitation.

3.1.6. Stopping conditions

The population will evolve until some stopping condition is satisfied. A simple stopping condition is to limit the number of iterations, *e.g.* that the evolution ends after a given number of generations. But the risk of setting the limit too low is that the algorithm will not have enough time to explore the search space. A superior stopping condition is to detect when the algorithm has converged, *e.g.* monitoring the best individual. If the best individual does not change from a given number of generation, we may say that the algorithm has converged. All components described in this section are dependent on this algorithm paradigm and will be described in detail more thoroughly the following sections.

3.2. MATHEMATICAL OPTIMIZATION

Mathematical optimization has the purpose of minimizing or maximizing some mathematical function f [14]. One wants to find the optimal combination of the input parameters that maximize or minimize the function, f.

3.2.1. Maxima and Mimima

The maximum/minimum values of a function f is known as the *extreme values* of f [15]. These extreme values are located at points where the slope of f change from positive to negative (or from negative to positive). If the domain of the function is a closed on a finite interval, the function may in addition have extreme values at the endpoints of f. Extreme values are divided into *local* and *global* values. The existence of a global value of the minimum/maximum of function f is defined in [15] as:

The function f has a global maximum value $f(x_0)$ at the point x_0 in its domain if

$$\forall x \in D_f: \mathrm{f}(x) \leq \mathrm{f}(x_0) \tag{3.2}$$

where D_f represents the domain of f. A function may have a global minimum value $f(x_1)$ at the point x_1 in its domain if

$$\forall x \in D_f : f(x) \geq f(x_1) \tag{3.3}$$

where D_f represents the domain of f. A function can at most have one *global* maximum or minimum value, but the value may occur in many points. The existence of local extreme values are defined in [15] as:

Function f has a local maximum value $f(x_0)$ at the point x_0 in its domain, provided there exists a number $h > 0$ such that

$$\forall x \in D_f, \exists h \in \mathbb{R} : \mathrm{f}(x) \leq \mathrm{f}(x_0) \wedge |\, x - x_0| < \mathrm{h} \tag{3.4}$$

and f has a local minimum value $f(x_1)$ at the point x_1 in its domain, provided there exists a number $h > 0$ such that

$$\forall x \in D_f, \exists h \in \mathbb{R} : f(x) \geq f(x_1) \wedge |x - x_1| < h. \tag{3.5}$$

Here R denotes the set of real numbers. We note that a global extreme value may also be a local extreme value, *i.e.* a global extreme value is the largest of all local extreme values [15]. Fig. (**3.1**) illustrates the occurrence of maxima and minima in a function f, denoted by the red line.

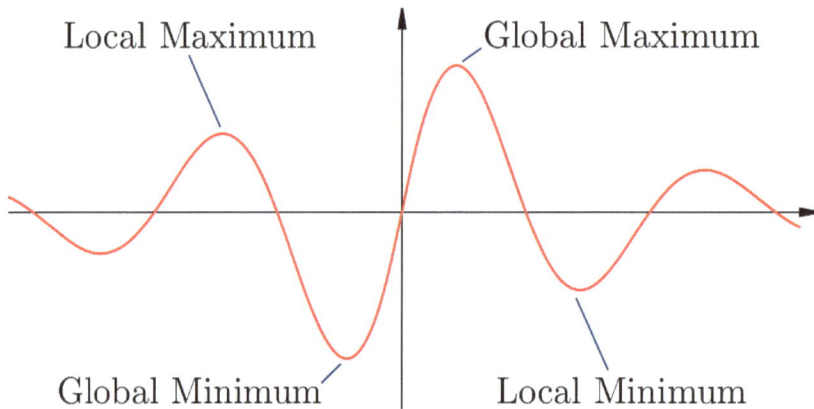

Fig. (3.1). Mathematical optimization - Maxima and Minima.

3.2.2. Optimization Problems

Optimization problems are divided into different categories based on problem characteristics:

- *Unconstrained problems:* Optimization of unconstrained problems does not set any restrictions on the input variables, *i.e.* the entire search space is feasible. When optimizing a function containing continuous values the only constraint is that each variable value is restricted to the domain of R.
- *Constrained problems:* Constrained problems define boundaries on the search space, meaning that a feasible solution of an optimization problem can only contain values that satisfy all constraints. For continuous values this means that only parts of the domain R contain feasible solutions to the optimization

problem.

- *Multi-objective problems:* These problems contain more than one objective to be optimized.
- *Multi-solution problems:* Multi-solution problems contain many optimal solutions, *e.g.* many reoccurring global extreme values and many local extreme values. The purpose when solving these problems, is to locate as many optimal solutions as possible.
- *Dynamic optimization problems:* The characteristics of these problems are that the objective function(s) changes over time, causing change in the position of the optimal values. One therefore has to develop methods to handle dynamic changes in the search space.

3.3. GENETIC ALGORITHMS

Genetic algorithms are possibly the first algorithms to model genetic evolution. The most important features of genetic algorithms are the selection operator and the crossover operator. The purpose of the selection operator is to simulate survival of the fittest, and crossover to simulate the ability of a population to reproduce itself. Algorithm **3.3.1** shows a generic genetic algorithm.

Algorithm 3.3.1 Pseudocode of a Genetic Algorithm

1: Generation counter $t = 0$;
2: Initialize population, $C(0)$, containing n invididuals;
3: **while** stopping conditions(s) is not true **do**
4:      Evaluate fitness of each individual, $x_i(t)$;
5:      Apply reproduction operators to create offsprings;
6:      Select new population, $C(t + 1)$;
7:      Advance to next generation $t = t + 1$;
8: **end while**

3.3.1. Crossover

Crossover operators are divided into categories based on the number of parents and how the genotype of individuals is represented. In terms of parents there are three types of crossover operators:

- *Asexual crossover* generates an offspring from only one parent individual.

- *Sexual crossover* generates up to two offsprings from two parents.
- *Multi-recombination crossover* where more than two parents are used to generate one or more offsprings.

Operators are also dependent on the genotype representation. For *binary representation* one usually apply a sexual crossover operator, creating an offspring, $\tilde{x}_1(t)$, from two parents, $x_1(t)$ and $x_2(t)$. The parameter t denotes áhe generation number. Sexual crossover could be done in three different ways:

- *One point Crossover*: Given two parents x_1 and x_2, each containing n_x genes, one randomly select a crossover point ε where $\varepsilon \in \{0, \dots, n_x\}$. The offspring $\tilde{x}_1(t)$ consists of a recombination of genotype from both parents, where

$$\tilde{x}_{1j}(t) = \begin{cases} x_{1j}(t), & \text{for } j = 0, \dots, \varepsilon \\ x_{2j}(t), & \text{for } j = (\varepsilon + 1), \dots, n_x. \end{cases} \qquad (3.6)$$

- *Two-point crossover*: This is similar to one-point crossover, but one selects two crossover points, ε_1 and ε_2. The offspring genotype will then consist of

$$\tilde{x}_{1j}(t) = \begin{cases} x_{1j}, & \text{for } j = 0, \dots, \varepsilon_1 \text{ or } j = (\varepsilon_2 + 1), \dots, n_x \\ x_{2j}, & \text{for } j = (\varepsilon_1 + 1), \dots, \varepsilon_2. \end{cases} \qquad (3.7)$$

- *Uniform crossover*: the probability p_x determines the genotype of the off- spring

$$\tilde{x}_{1j}(t) = \begin{cases} x_{1j}(t), & \text{if } p_x \leq \text{ a randomly generated number in range } [0,1] \\ x_{2j}(t), & \text{otherwise.} \end{cases} \qquad (3.8)$$

where $j \in \{0, \dots, n_x\}$.

These methods could also be used when producing two offsprings by adding genes that are not chosen for the first offspring to be added to the second offspring. One could also adapt these methods to *floating-point representations*. When simulating evolution it is important to add some randomness when applying reproduction operators. This is because we want to simulate the fact that it is not been given in any specie the individuals are able to reproduce. Reproduction operators are applied to selected parents by some probability, p_c.

3.3.2. Mutation

By introducing mutation one adds diversity to the population. Crossover produce individuals based on the genetic combination of their parents, resulting in offsprings that are very similar to their parent. By adding a mutation operator one helps individuals to explore the entire search space.

Like crossover, mutation operators are organized into groups in terms of their gene representation. For *binary* representations, the examples are:

- *Uniform mutation*: gene indices of a chromosome are chosen at random and negated.
- *Inorder mutation*: one selects two indices and only the genes between these indices may be selected for uniform mutation.

For *floating-point representation*, Michalewicz [16] introduced a non-uniform mutation operator. The *j*th gene of chromosome $x_{ij}(t)$ is selected for mutation. The mutated gene, $\grave{x}_{ij}(t)$ is defined as

$$\grave{x}_{ij}(t) = \begin{cases} x_{ij}(t) + \Delta(t, UP - x_{ij}(t)) & \text{if a random number is 0} \\ x_{ij}(t) - \Delta(t, x_{ij}(t) - LB) & \text{if a random number is 1} \end{cases} \quad \textbf{(3.9)}$$

where *UP* is the upper bound of the *j*th gene, and *LB* is the lowest bound of *j*. $\Delta(t, y)$ will return a random number in the range of $[t, y]$. As the generation number *t* grows, results in a smaller value for $\Delta(t, y)$ and smaller mutation steps, which corresponds with the principle of moving the focus from exploration to exploitation as the population grows older. As with crossover the mutation operator is applied to each gene with a probability of p_m, known as the mutation rate p_m.

3.3.3. Control Parameters

Control parameters are parameters that affect the performance of the algorithm. The performance of a genetic algorithm is highly dependent on the population size, crossover rate and mutation rate. Finding the best values of these parameters is an optimization problem in itself so various strategies have been proposed. The effect of a larger population is described in Section 3.1. Early studies proposed large values of the crossover rate and relatively low value of the mutation rate, and that these should be kept constant. However, later studies have shown that optimal values of the control parameters could improve performance significantly. Therefore, dynamically changing these parameters could be more beneficial. An example is to proportionally reduce the mutation rate when the generation number increases to favor exploration in early generations. Another strategy is to apply the mutation operator on individuals, based on their fitness level. This means that the mutation probability should be higher of individuals with a low fitness level in order to move them into more promising areas of the search space.

3.4. GENETIC PROGRAMMING

Genetic programming focuses on the evolution of geno-types (see Section 3.1). The difference lies in the representation scheme used for individuals, where in genetic programming trees are used to represent the individuals. This paradigm was first introduced by evolving computer programs, where an individual represents a part of the program. To measure the fitness of the individuals, each computer program is executed, and the fitness level represents then the performance for solving the problem.

3.4.1. Tree Based Representation

To represent computer programs by using trees one has to define a set of rules and operators that reflects the problem domain. This set is known as the *grammar*. The grammar is a super set that contains a terminal set, defining legal variables and constants; a function set containing legal operators and a set of semantic rules. Individuals can be of different size (depth of the tree), form (number of branches) and complexity. Fig. (**3.2**) shows two examples of tree-based representations, where individuals are mathematical expressions.

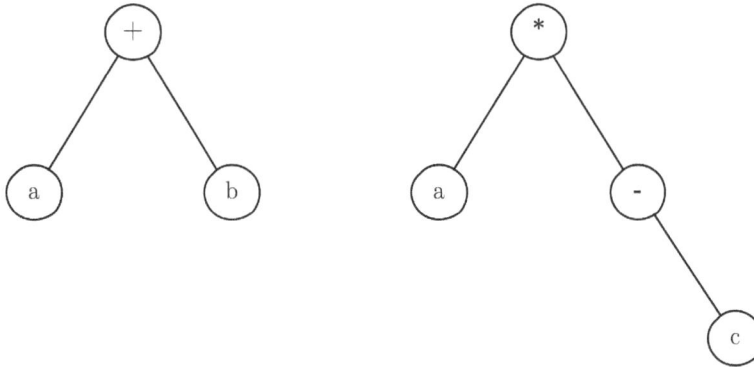

Fig. (3.2). Examples of tree-based individuals.

3.4.2. Fitness Function

When calculating fitness, each the program is executed on some test cases. If the individuals are represented by mathematical expressions, the fitness level may be determined by the number of correct calculations based on some training set. This is similar to the approach used in supervised learning, where the training set consists of input patterns and corresponding target values.

3.4.3. Crossover Operators

Crossover in genetic programming is recombination of trees. Given two individuals, crossover may then be achieved by selecting a subtree in both individuals and then swapping them.

3.4.4. Mutation Operators

Some proposed mutation operators are:

- *Function node mutation*: Randomly selecting an operator from the function set, with the same *arity*, to replace a function of the individual.
- *Terminal node mutation*: Randomly replacing a leaf node with another leaf node from the terminal set.
- *Swap mutation*: Randomly selecting a sub-tree and swapping children of the root node.
- *Grow mutation*: Randomly selecting a node and replacing it with a randomly generated tree.

3.5. EVOLUTIONARY PROGRAMMING

Instead of evolving genetic material *Evolutionary programming* focus on *phenotypic* evolution; that means the evolution of behaviour. This means that there is no exchange of genetic material between individuals, *i.e.* no crossover is applied in the algorithm. Mutation and selection is used. Evolutionary programming was first developed to evolve *finite state machines* with the purpose of finding a set of optimal behaviours within a space of observable behaviours. Since the fitness level of behaviour is dependent on the rest of available behaviours, a relative fitness level has been introduced. Selection is based on competition where individuals with high fitness level have a higher probability of being chosen for the next generation.

3.5.1. Representation

Individuals are represented by a tuple

$$\mathcal{X}_i(t) = (x_i(t), \sigma_i(t)) \tag{3.10}$$

where $x_i(t)$ represents the genetic material of the ith individual, and $\sigma_i(t)$ represents the *strategy parameter*, determining the behaviour of the individual.

3.5.2. Mutation Operators

Mutation is defined as:

$$x'_{ij}(t) = x_{ij}(t) + \Delta x_{ij}(t) \tag{3.11}$$

where the offspring $x'_{ij}(t)$ is generated by adding a mutation step, $\Delta x_{ij}(t)$, to the parent $x_{ij}(t)$. Mutation step size may also be known as *noise*. The mutation step size is calculated as

$$\Delta x_{ij}(t) = \Phi(\sigma_{ij}(t))\eta_{ij}(t) \tag{3.12}$$

where the scaling factor Φ determines in what degree the added noise, $\eta_{ij}(t)$, should affect the offspring. The only way to introduce new genetic material into the population is by applying the mutation operator. This implies that it is crucial in terms of performance to consider the *exploration-exploitation* trade-off . As for all evolutionary algorithms one wants to make large mutation steps in early generations to promote exploration of the search space. In later generations, after gaining information about the search space, one wants to move individuals into promising areas of the search space, making small mutation steps to promote exploitation. This trade-off is determined by the values of the strategy parameter σ, since this value affect the scaling factor Φ. Based on the scaling factor, evolutionary algorithms are grouped into three categories:

- *Non-adaptive*: the scaling factor is linear, $\Phi(\sigma) = \sigma$.
- *Dynamic*: the step size changes over time by using some deterministic function for Φ.
- *Self-adaptive*: step size changes dynamically, where the best values of the strategy parameter are learned in a parallel process.

There are various ways of choosing the amount of noise η_{ij} to be added when creating an offspring. The *uniform distribution* is an example of this:

$$\eta_{ij}(t) \sim U(x_{min,j}, x_{max,j}) \tag{3.13}$$

where noise is sampled from a uniform distribution U within some predefined boundary x_{min} and x_{max}. Then amount of noise $\eta_{ij}(t)$ is a randomly chosen value within the interval $[x_{min,j}, x_{max,j}]$ The notation $X \sim$ means that the variable X has a probability distribution. A uniform probability distribution means that all values in the interval have the same probability of being selected, illustrated in Fig. (**3.3**) In [17] a mutation operator based on a standard uniform distribution was proposed where all individuals make random movements towards the best individual in the population, defined as

$$\Delta x_{ij}(t) = U(0,1)(y_j'(t) - x_{ij}(t)) \tag{3.14}$$

where $y'(t)$ denotes the best individual in the population, and $U(0, 1)$ is a random number sampled from the uniform distribution of $[0, 1]$.

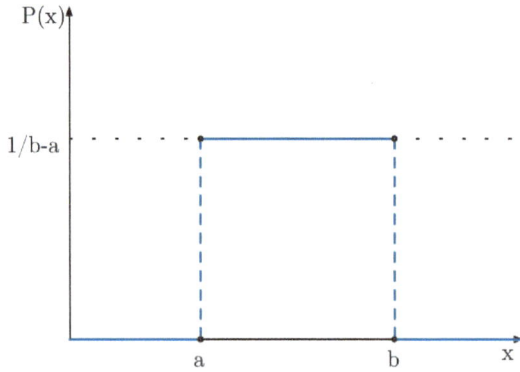

Fig. (3.3). Uniform distribution with boundaries *a* and *b*.

3.5.3. Selection Operators

The selection operator is used when selecting individuals to survive to the next generation. The selection process is based on competition, where both parents and offspring compete. The actual competition occurs when calculating the relative fitness score of each individual. The relative fitness score, denoted as $s_i(t)$ for individual $x_i(t)$, is calculated as

$$s_i(t) = \sum_{l=1}^{n_P} s_{il}(t) \tag{3.15}$$

where n_P is a number of randomly selected competitors from the population. $s_{il}(t)$ is calculated as

$$s_{il}(t) = \begin{cases} 1, & \text{if the absolute fitness level of } x_i \text{ is higher than of } x_l. \\ 0, & \text{otherwise} \end{cases} \tag{3.16}$$

After calculating the relative fitness score any selection operator could be used for selecting individuals for the next generation:

- *Elitism*: μ individuals with the best relative fitness score are selected for the next generation.

- *Tournament*: n individuals are randomly selected and the individual with the highest fitness level survives to the next generation. This is applied until all individuals are selected.
- *Proportional*: each individual is assigned a probability p_s of being selected. Roulette wheel selection can be used to select individuals. The selection process is similar to spinning a roulette wheel where the size of each field is proportional to the probability value of each individual, *i.e.* individuals with higher probability value have a higher probability of being selected.

3.6. EVOLUTION STRATEGIES

This paradigm came from the observation that biological processes are optimized through evolution. Evolution is a biological process, which implies that the evolution optimizes itself. This observation leads to the *Evolution strategies* paradigm, that tries not only to optimize the genetic material of an individual, but also its behaviour. Like evolutionary programming, described in section 3.5, an individual is represented by a tuple consisting of both genotype and phenotype. Another feature of this paradigm is that mutated individuals are only accepted if it improves the fitness level of the individuals undergoing mutation.

3.6.1. Generic Evolution Strategies Algorithm

The main components of the algorithm are:

- *Initialization:* create individuals and initialize both genotype and strategy parameter for each individual.
- *Crossover:* the crossover operator is applied on at least two parents, where both genotype and strategy parameters are recombined, creating an off- spring.
- *Mutation:* offspring created by the crossover operator are mutated based on the individual strategy parameter.
- *Evaluation:* individuals are evaluated based on genotypic material where an absolute fitness measure is used.
- *Selection:* selection operators are used to select individuals for crossover and for selecting individuals to survive for the next generation.

3.6.2. Strategy Parameter

The *strategy parameter* is *self-adaptive*, meaning that through the evolution of individuals the strategy parameter will fine-tune itself so that maximum search progress is obtained. The self-adapted strategy parameter defines the best behaviour for each individual in terms of direction and step size.

3.6.3. Selection Operator

The selection operator is used to select parents for crossover and select individuals to survive for the next generation. For every generation, μ parents produce λ offspring. The λ offspring is then mutated. Two strategies have been developed for selecting the next generation:

- $(\mu + \lambda)$: both parents and offsprings compete for survival. μ parents generate λ offsprings, where $1 \leq \mu \leq \lambda < .\infty$ The μ best individuals from the set containing μ parents and λ offsprings are selected for the next generation. Elitism is used.
- (μ, λ): μ parents generate λ offspring, where $1 \leq \mu < \lambda < \infty$. μ individuals are selected from λ offspring for the next generation. Elitism is not used.

3.6.4. Crossover Operators

Two types of crossover operators are proposed:

- *Local crossover:* two parents are randomly selected to generate one offspring.
- *Global crossover:* more than two randomly selected parents generate one offspring. As more parents are using it, the more divergent the offspring becomes. This method favours exploration when a large number of parents is used.

Recombination in both *local* and *global* crossover can be done by a *discrete* or *intermediate* way. By using discrete recombination each component of both the genotype and the strategy parameter of the offspring are randomly selected from one of the parents. Intermediate recombination will produce an offspring where each component is a weighted average of the corresponding component from all parents.

3.6.5. Mutation Operator

Offspring are mutated with a probability of 1. The mutation is done in two steps where (1) the strategy parameter self-adapts and (2) based on the adapted strategy parameter, the genotype of the individuals is mutated.

3.7. DIFFERENTIAL EVOLUTION

Information about the current population is valuable in terms of guiding the search to more attractive parts of the search domain. By letting the candidate solutions of an optimization problem evolve, the solutions will ideally approach another. This is because the individuals are attracted to parts of the search space that assigns them a high fitness level. Large distances between individuals indicates a young generation and individuals want to make large mutation steps to explore the search domain. Small distances indicate that individuals have moved to good parts of the search space, arguing that the mutation step size should be small to focus on exploitation. Instead of sampling the step size from a uniform probability function, as in section 3.3, the step size may be influenced by the distance between the individuals.

3.7.1. Mutation Operator

For every individual $x_i(t)$ in the current population, the mutation operator generates a *trail vector*. The trail vector is composed of a target vector, selected from the population by some selection operator, a difference vector, depicting the distance between two randomly selected individuals from the population, and a scaling factor β. The trial vector is defined as

$$u_i(t) = x_{i_1}(t) + \beta(x_{i_2}(t) - x_{i_3}(t)) \qquad (3.17)$$

where $i \neq i_1 \neq i_2 \neq i_3$ and $\beta \in (0, \infty)$. In other words, the trial vector is constructed by mutating a target vector based on the difference or distance between two randomly selected individuals. A large distance will result in a large mutation step of the target vector. Both $x_i(t)$ and $u_i(t)$ are used to create offsprings by using the crossover operator, described in the next paragraph.

3.7.2. Crossover Operator

The crossover operator recombines the trial vector, described in equation 3.17, and the corresponding parent vector $x_i(t)$ as follows

$$
x'_{ij}(t) = \begin{cases} u_{ij}(t) & \text{if } j \in J \\ x_{ij}(t) & \text{otherwise.} \end{cases} \tag{3.18}
$$

where $x_{ij}(t)$ describes the jth gene of individual i, and J is a set of crossover indices. If j is in set J, then the jth value of the offspring x' is assigned the jth value of the trial vector. Otherwise, it is assigned the jth value of the parent vector. The indix members of J can be randomly selected from n_x possible crossover points, where each index varies from 1, ... , n_x, and has the same probability p_r of being chosen for J. The size of J and the influence of the trial vector has on the offspring, is dependent on the the value of p_r. This is known as *Binomial Crossover*.

3.7.3. Selection

Random selection is used for selecting individuals for calculating the difference vector in Equation 3.17. For selecting the target vector one could also use random selection, or one could always pick the best individual. To select individuals for the next generation, we use *Deterministic selection*, which means that an offspring will only replace its parent if it has a higher fitness level.

3.7.4. Control Parameters

The population size, the scale factor β and the probability value p_r, used in the crossover operator, are control parameters that affect performance of the algorithm. The size of the population influences exploration where a larger population means a higher diversity, *i.e.* more individuals to choose from when calculating the trial vector. However, the computational complexity increase for each generation, with the size of the population. The scaling factor determines the size of the mutation steps where smaller values generate smaller step size, resulting in slower convergence. Larger values of the probability value for crossover will increase diversity and exploration, resulting in faster convergence time.

3.8. CULTURAL ALGORITHMS

Like the differential evolutionary algorithms, described in section 3.7, *Cultural algorithms* use information about the search space to guide the individuals of the population into promising areas of the search space. What makes the algorithm different from other evolutionary algorithms is that it uses the culture of a population to guide its individuals to promising areas. In [13] various definitions of culture are presented, where the culture is described as the total sum of all behaviour learned by the individuals of a population. The culture may be considered as tradition and is inherited from generation to generation.

In computational intelligence, culture may be interpreted as data that affects the behaviour of individuals of a population, *i.e.* how they are moved around in the search space. The algorithm contains two search spaces, the population space containing genetic information about individuals and their fitness, and the belief space, containing cultural information about the population. Fig. (**3.4**) illustrates two spaces, and the communication between them. Algorithm **3.8.1** outlines a general cultural algorithm. Each component of the algorithm is explained in the next paragraphs.

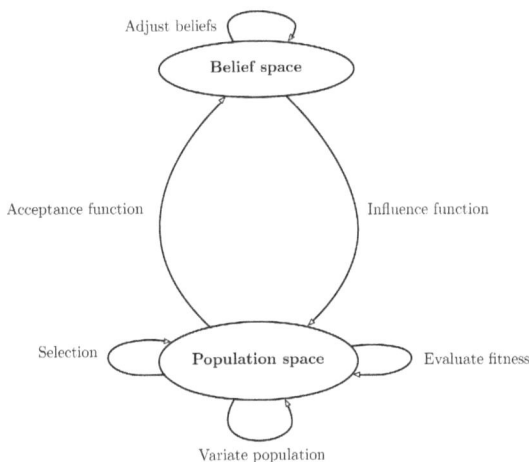

Fig. (3.4). The figure shows the population and belief space of a Cultural Algorithms.

Algorithm 3.8.1 Pseudocode of a Cultural algorithm

Set the generation number counter, $t = 0$;
Create and initialize the population space, $\mathcal{C}(0)$;
Create and initialize the belief space, $\mathcal{B}(0)$;
while Stopping condition is not true **do**
    Evaluate the fitness of each individual $x_i(t) \in \mathcal{C}(t)$;
    Adjust $\mathcal{B}(t)$ based on result of some acceptance function $A(\mathcal{C}(t))$;
    Variate the population $\mathcal{C}(t)$ by applying some influence function $I(\mathcal{B}(t))$;
    $t = t + 1$
    Select the new population
end while

3.8.1. Belief Space

The belief space is a knowledge database that containing generalization of optimal behaviour of the individuals, and evolves from generation to generation. The behavioural pattern of individuals are represented by *knowledge components*. In general, the belief space consists of at least two components:

- *Situational* components contain information about the best individual, that is the best solution of the optimization problem up to this point.
- *Normative* components contain mutation guidelines, *i.e.* intervals in each dimension describing good areas of the search space.

These components are represented by the tuple

$$\mathcal{B}(t) = (\mathcal{S}(t), \mathcal{N}(t)) \tag{3.19}$$

where $S(t)$ denotes the situational component and $N(t)$ denotes the normative component; t denotes the number of generations. One could also add these components, see [13]:

- *Domain* components are similar to situational components, but differ by keeping an archive of the best individuals in every population.
- *Topographical* components containing a multi-dimensional matrix representing the search space, and having the purpose to guide the search into unexplored areas.

3.8.2. Acceptance Function

The acceptance function is used to select which individuals are going to shape the belief space. There exist static selection methods, *i.e.* selecting the top 10 percent best individuals. One could also use dynamic methods where the number of selected individuals are changing from generation to generation. An example of a dynamic method is the number of selected individuals of each generation, to favor the exploitation of the search process for later iterations.

3.8.3. Influence Function

The individuals selected by the acceptance function shape the belief space, creating a belief template for adjusting all individuals of the population towards global beliefs. This is done by applying the *influence function* on each individual of the population. By using its knowledge components, the belief space dictates the mutation steps and their direction. The influence function then moves individuals around in the search space based on these beliefs. There are four ways of applying the knowledge components of the influence function:

- Only normative components are used when producing an offspring.
- Only situational components are used when selecting the direction of the mutation of individuals.
- Normative components are used to determine the step size, situational ones are used to define the direction.
- Normative components are used to determine both the step size and the directions.

CHAPTER 4

System Specification

Abstract: The system requirements are divided into two types, functional and non-functional. Both of them are described in addition to their data visualization.

Keywords: Functional requirement, Non-functional requirements, System objective.

4.1. INTRODUCTION

The purpose of this chapter is to describe the objective of the system, including requirements and constraints that the system must satisfy. *System requirements* depicts the services that the system must provide and its operational constraints [18]. It should give a detailed description of the functionality that will be implemented, but one should avoid the discussion of specific design choices or implementation. System requirements are divided into two subcategories:

• Functional requirements
• Non-functional requirements

Functional requirements describe the requirements of each service that the system provides, and also the input/output of each service. They should reflect the customers' expectations of the system. Imprecision in the requirements may result in systems that fail to meet the needs of the customer, mainly because the developer misinterpreted the requirements [18]. The description of the functional requirements should contain enough details to avoid misinterpretation, without defining any boundaries on the implementation. *Non-functional requirements* do not describe requirements of a specific functionality, but for the system as a whole. However, the requirements define constraints on the properties of the system. Examples are security requirements, system performance requirements and reliability requirements. There is one important characteristic that makes the functional and the non-functional requirements be different: A system that violates a functional requirement may still be usable, but a system that violates a non-functional is not. For instance, if a web browser should be able to display both text and images (its functional requirement), but fails to display images, the user is still able to display text using the web browser. However, if an air traffic control system fails to meet its security and reliability requirements, it should never be used for air traffic control.

We want to be able to verify the requirements of the system. A requirement stating that the user interface needs to be simple is a poor requirement because it is difficult to test [18]. Therefore, one should restate the requirement to make it quantifiable, *e.g. "the total number of errors of an experienced user should not exceed two per day"*. The *functional* and *non-functional requirements* of the system is presented in Section 4.3 and 4.4, respectively, and in Section 4.2 the *system objective* is described.

4.2. SYSTEM OBJECTIVE

The main objective of the system is to analyse and visualize high-dimensional data, with the purpose of revealing underlying structures that otherwise would be hard to identify. Through visualization one presents the data in a manner that makes it easier for experts to further analyse them. The system provides two evolutionary clustering algorithms to analyse the data, where each one employs a different paradigm of *Evolutionary algorithms* to optimize the *K-means algorithm*.

The cluster analysis should not be dependent on any pre-defined information about the clustering structures to be able to analyse data. An increasing number of dimensions introduce restrictions on how one can visualize the data in a meaningful way. Thus, the system needs to provide a visualization regime that can handle high-dimensional data.

4.3. FUNCTIONAL REQUIREMENTS

4.3.1. System Input

The system should be able to import data from a text file. Each line of the text file represents a data object. The attributes of each data object must be separated by either a "," or a *whitespace*. The relevant attributes must be *numerical*. Some data sets contain meta-information about the data objects in leading and/or trailing attributes. Hence, one should be able to ignore when importing them into the system. An example is the *Iris* data set (See Section 8.3.2), where the last attribute represents which of the Iris flower the data object belongs to. This information is a result of a classification process conducted on the data, and should be ignored, since it is not a feature of the original data (See Fig. **4.1**). The text file can be any ASCII file, as long as the data match the format presented earlier.

```
5.1,3.5,1.4,0.2,Iris-setosa
4.9,3.0,1.4,0.2,Iris-setosa
4.7,3.2,1.3,0.2,Iris-setosa
4.6,3.1,1.5,0.2,Iris-setosa
5.0,3.6,1.4,0.2,Iris-setosa
5.4,3.9,1.7,0.4,Iris-setosa
4.6,3.4,1.4,0.3,Iris-setosa
5.0,3.4,1.5,0.2,Iris-setosa
4.4,2.9,1.4,0.2,Iris-setosa
```

Fig. (4.1). Data representation of the Iris data set.

4.3.2. Cluster Analysis

The user should be able to select which of the algorithms to do the clustering process and also adjust the specific parameters of the algorithm (*e.g. population size, maximum number of generations, maximum size of individuals, etc.*). In addition, the user should be able to select evolutionary operators and adjust their parameters (*e.g.mutation and crossover rate etc.*). After selecting and initializing the algorithms, the user should be able to perform the cluster analysis. After the analysis is finished, the user should be able to import new data sets, and re-initialize algorithms and the operators without the need to reboot the system.

4.3.3. Visualization

The resulting clustering structure should be visualized so the user can further:

1. analyse the correctness of the clustering structure.
2. analyse the groupings of data.

The data undergoing analysis may be of different dimensions. As a result, the system should be able to provide a visual presentation of the data, of any dimension.

4.4. NON-FUNCTIONAL REQUIREMENTS

4.4.1. Functional Correctness

A requirement of the system is that different components behave as expected. This means that given some input to a component, the output from it should correspond to the expected output. For instance, if we provide two data objects to an algorithm that calculate Euclidean distance (See Eq. 2.5), we may expect, for instance, that the output from this algorithm is the correct Euclidean distance between the objects.

4.4.2. Extensibility

The architecture of the system should facilitate extensibility. By introducing new functionality, such as additional evolutionary algorithms or evolutionary operators, should not require alterations of the existing features. This implies that the different components of the system need to satisfy the *re-usability* requirements to minimize the effort of adding additional features. For instance, some paradigms of evolutionary algorithms employ the same evolutionary operators. Then, these operators should be reusable.

4.4.3. Maintainability

Maintainability suggests a low level of coupling between different components of the system to make future maintenance more simple. For instance, the design of the system should make it easy to identify broken components, and to correct them without the need to change the sound components.

4.4.4. Portability

The system should be platform independent, meaning that one should be able to run the system on different platforms.

4.4.1. Usability

The user interface should be intuitive. It should be easy for the user to understand how to import data to the system, initialize the algorithm parameters, run the cluster analysis, *etc.*

CHAPTER 5

Design and Implementation

Abstract: In this chapter, the system architecture and different tools that have been used in the implementation process such as Netbeans and JavaFX, are described.

Keywords: Complexity of K-means algorithm, Davies-Bouldin Index, Evolutionary operators, Fitness evaluation, Genetic Algorithm, Junit, JavaFX, K-means algorithm, Maven, Netbeans.

5.1. INTRODUCTION

In this chapter, we describe the design and implementation of the system:

- In Section 5.2 one describes the architecture and different design patterns employed in the development of the system.
- Section 5.3 describes the tools employed in the development of the system.
- Section 5.4 deals with the internal data structure used to represent imported data of the system, and the implementation of the *K-means clustering algorithm*.
- Section 5.5 describes two evolutionary clustering algorithms.

The time-complexity of the algorithms are also analysed using *Big-O notation* [19].

5.2. SYSTEM ARCHITECTURE

Fig. (**5.1**) shows a *high-level* representation of the system architecture, where relationships and dependencies between classes are illustrated. The system is designed to satisfy the *Model-View-Controller* (MVC) architectural pattern to separate the User Interface (UI) and business logic. The controller classes and view classes of MVC are marked with pink. The MVC pattern is further described in Chapter 7. The classes marked with blue constitute the *Evolutionary Clustering algorithms* (ECA) (Section 5.5), the green classes represent the *K-Means algorithm* and its components (Section 5.4.2), and the orange represents the utility classes, *i.e.* classes for importing and representing data in the system (Section 5.4.1).

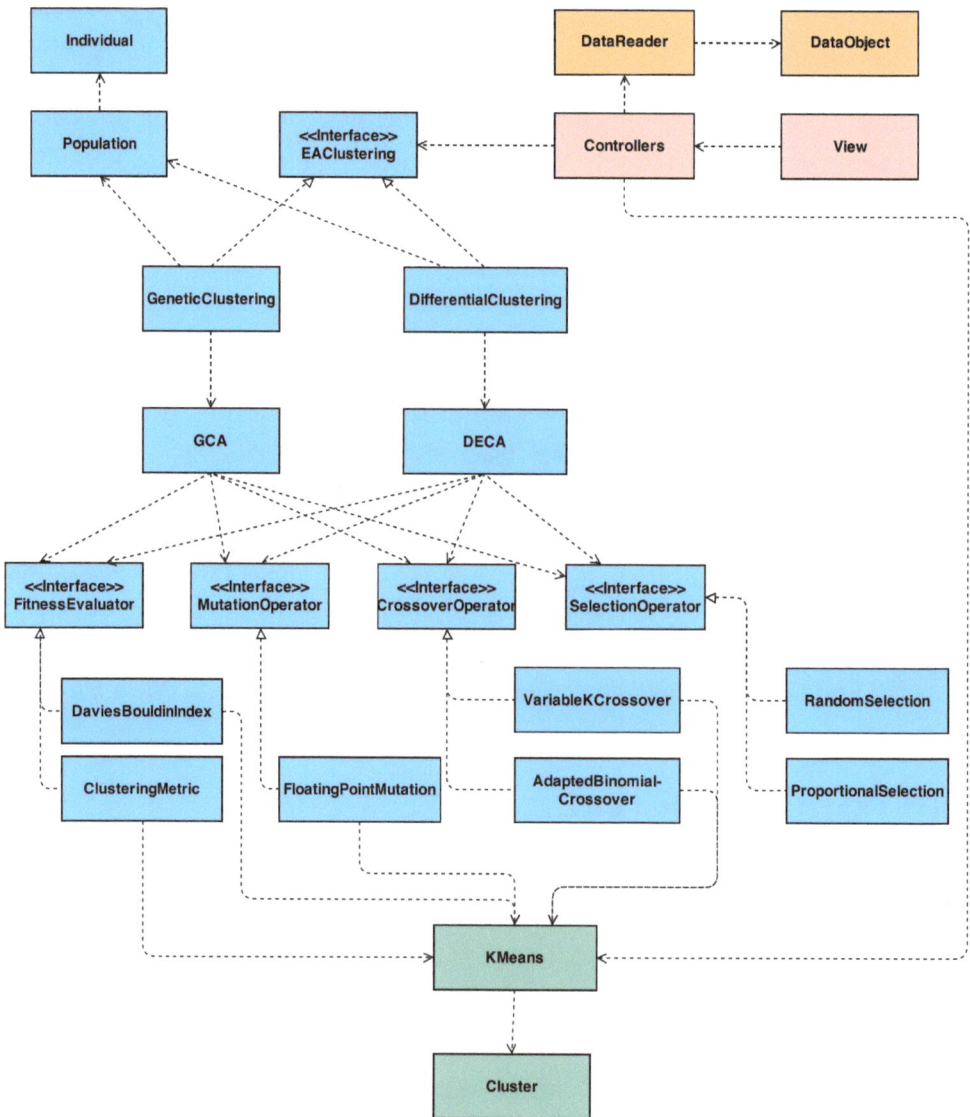

Fig. (5.1). UML diagram of the high-level architecture of the system.

5.2.1. Dependency Injection

The evolutionary clustering algorithms (ECA) are dependent on different evolutionary operators, such as mutation operators, selection operators and crossover operators. To make the ECAs loosely coupled from the operators, we pass a reference to each operator through the ECAs constructor, rather than creating the dependencies in the respective ECA. This is known as *Dependency Injection (DI)* pattern. For instance, the user specifies which of the available fitness evaluation methods he wants to employ in the relative ECA through the user interface. An instance of the selected fitness evaluation method is then created by the controller class instead of being created in the ECA, and as a result the ECA does not need to know anything about the fitness evaluation method. Fig. (**5.2**) illustrates an example of how the DI pattern is employed in our sys-tem. In this example, the user wants to employ the *Davies-Bouldin Index (DBI)* (Section 5.5.6) as a fitness evaluator of the *Genetic Clustering algorithm (GCA)*. The controller creates an instance of DBI and pass this object down to the GCA. The same case is illustrated in Fig. (**5.3**), but without the DI pattern. In this case, the GCA relies on knowledge about DBI to be able to create an instance of it. If we are going to alter the DBI, we must also update the GCA based on the alteration made to the DBI. In reference to the *maintainability* requirement of Section 4.4, developers can alter the DBI without the need to alter the GCA. Thus, making the system easier to maintain. Note that the DI pattern is employed for all evolutionary operators used in the ECA.

5.2.2. Open-Closed Principle

To be able to extend the system in the future with additional evolutionary operators or fitness evaluation methods, it is important that relevant components conform to the *Open-Closed Principle (OCP)* [20]. By conforming to the OCP, we create components that are *open* for extension and *closed* for modification. This can be achieved through *abstraction* [20]. In the system architecture presented earlier, the behaviour of the ECAs is closed for modification since they depend on the fixed behaviour of the evolutionary operators and the fitness evaluator, defined by their respective interfaces. At the same time, the behaviour of the ECAs is extendible by creating new derivatives of the different interfaces.

For instance, in order to add new fitness evaluation methods to the system we just create a derivative of the *Fitness Evaluator*-interface (see Fig. **5.1**). In this way we are extending the behaviour of the ECA without the need to modify it.

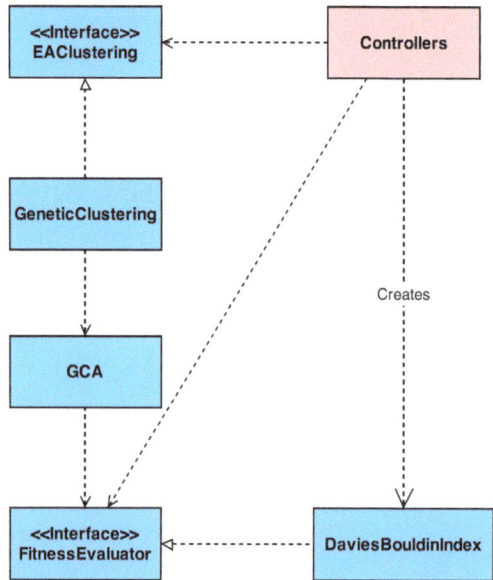

Fig. (5.2). Example of architecture with dependency injection.

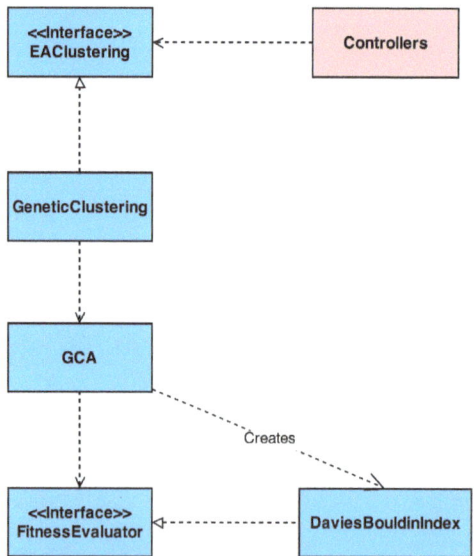

Fig. (5.3). Example of architecture without dependency injection.

5.3. TOOLS AND TECHNOLOGIES

This section will give an overview of the different technologies and tools used in the development of the system.

5.3.1. Java

Because of its portability *Java* was selected as programming language.

5.3.2. JavaFX

JavaFX is a software platform for creating *Java* applications [21]. JavaFX conforms to the Model-View-Controller (MVC) pattern, where the user interface is separated from the business logic by using *FXML*. JavaFX and the MVC are described in more detail in chapter 7.

5.3.3. Netbeans

Because of its support for JavaFX, *Netbeans IDE* was selected as development environment.

5.3.4. Maven

Maven is a build management tool for software development [22]. The purpose of Maven is to make the project portable. Maven handles all project dependencies, for instance by automatically downloading external libraries (and specific versions) on which that the project is dependent.

5.3.5. Git and GitHub

Git is a distributed revision control system that lets you store versions of your project in both local and remote repositories [23]. A private repository on *GitHub* was used as a remote repository [24].

5.3.6. JUnit

To conduct unit tests we have employed *JUnit* [25], a framework for creating unit tests for Java applications. Unit tests verify the functional correctness (See Section 4.4.1) of each component of the system.

5.4. DATA STRUCTURE AND CLUSTERING

In this section we describe the implementation of the functionality to import data to the system and also a description of how the data is represented in the system.

5.4.1. Import Data and Data Structure

To import data into the system we have created a utility class known as *DataReader*. Based on the constraints defined in Section 4.3, each line of the imported file represents a pattern of the data set. DataReader reads each line of the file, and creates a *DataObject* to represent each pattern in the system. A DataObject has a given number of attributes, each representing a feature of the pattern. From the functional requirements of Section 4.3, data objects of some data sets contain meta-information in leading/trailing attributes, and the user should be able to specify which of the attributes that contains the actual data. This is achieved by providing an interval of indices $[i, ... j]$ to the DataReader, where $0 \geq i, j < n$ and n is the actual number of attributes. Only attributes relative to this interval will be employed to create data objects.

From the system specification one requirement was that the data type of attributes must be numerical. However, we want to create a data structure that could store data objects independent of the relative data type, thus making the system more extendible to handle additional data types of the features. The attributes of DataObjects are therefore represented as *strings* in the system. In *Java*, any data type has a String representation, making it trivial to convert from String to any data type when needed. As a result, we only have to be concerned with the data types of attributes in classes that manipulate attributes.

5.4.2. K-means Algorithm

The structure of the implemented *K-means algorithm* follows the outline of Algorithm **2.1.1**. First, we initialize K clusters by randomly selecting K distinct DataObjects from the imported data set to act as centroids for each K cluster. After initializing all clusters, the algorithm groups the imported data by assigning each DataObject to the closest centroid based on *Euclidean distance*. Clustering of the data is illustrated in Algorithm **5.4.1**.

Algorithm 5.4.1 K-Means algorithm: data clustering

1: *closest* ← pointer to the closest cluster
2: **for all** *DataObject* of the imported data set **do**
3:     *closestDistance* ← distance to closest cluster
4:     **for all** clusters *c* **do**
5:         Calculate *distance* from *DataObject* to cluster *c*   ▷ see Alg. 5.4.2
6:         **if** *distance* is less than *closestDistance* **then**
7:             Update *closestDistance* ← *distance*
8:             Update *closest* ← *c*
9:         **end if**
10:     **end for**
11:     Add *DataObject* to *closest*
12: **end for**

Algorithm 5.4.2 K-Means algorithm: Euclidean distance between objects

---

Require: size of *DataObject* and *centroid* has to be equal.
1: *sum* ← summation value
2: **for** the size of *centroid* **do**
3:     Subtract the *i*th attribute of *centroid* and *DataObject*
4:     Multiply the resulting value by itself (power of 2) and add it to *sum*
5: **end for**
6: **return** square root of *sum*

After the clustering step is done, one needs to compute new centroids for each cluster. For each cluster, the new centroid is calculated as in Equation 2.12. Note that we are only computing the new centroid once when running the K-means algorithm in our system. The reason for this is that we employ evolutionary algorithm to optimize the K-means algorithm, thus subsequently optimize the positioning of the K cluster centroids. The idea is to let the evolutionary algorithm be responsible of finding the optimal positioning of the K cluster centroids. In a standard K-means algorithm, illustrated in Algorithm **2.1.1**, one find the optimal positioning of K centroids by re-clustering the data objects and updating cluster centroids until all centroids are constant.

Each time these operations are performed, we add $O(n^2 \cdot d) + O(n \cdot d)$ to the time-complexity of the algorithm (See next paragraph). Also, the number of iterations required to make the algorithm converge may become quite high. The benefits in terms of reduced time-complexity will become evident in Section 5.5, which describes the time-complexity of the ECAs. Here we see that the clustering of the data is one of the heaviest operations in ECAs. Thus, we want to keep this operation as light as possible.

Complexity of K-Means Operations

The time-complexity of the K-means operation applied in our system is as follows:

- **Clustering of data objects:** n data objects are assigned to the closest of k clusters. To find the closest cluster of a data object, we need to calculate the Euclidean distance from the data object to each of the cluster centroids. This has the time complexity of $O(k \cdot d)$, where k is the number of clusters, and d is the number of dimensions of the data. For each of the n data objects the time-complexity is of $O(n \cdot k \cdot d)$. In worst case, the size of k is equal to n/2 . This gives the time complexity of $O(n^2 \cdot d)$.

- **Computing new centroid:** To update the centroid of a cluster we first compute the sum of cluster members. Calculating the sum of two data objects has the time-complexity of $O(d)$. As a result, calculating the sum of all cluster members has time-complexity of $O(n \cdot d)$, since the number of members in a cluster is equal to n in worst case (all data objects are a member of the same cluster). Next, we divide the produced sum by the number of members, that has the time-complexity of $O(d)$. The resulting time-complexity of computing the new centroid of a cluster is $O(n \cdot d) + O(d) = O(n \cdot d)$. We compute a new centroid for each of the k clusters. This yields the time-complexity of $O(k \cdot n \cdot d)$. As before, in worst case, the number of clusters is equal to $n/2$. This means that $k = n/2$ clusters only have one member besides the cluster centroid, resulting in complexity of $O(1 \cdot d)$ to compute the new centroid per cluster k. This means that the total time-complexity of computing a new centroid for all clusters is $O(n \cdot d)$.

5.5. EVOLUTIONARY ALGORITHMS

5.5.1. Genetic Clustering Algorithm

In this section we describe the design and implementation of a *Genetic Clustering Algorithm* (GCA), where a *Genetic algorithm* is applied to a the standard *K-means algorithm*. The purpose of this algorithm is to find the optimal value of K for a given data set that yields an optimal clustering structure based on some fitness measure. Individuals can have different chromosome size. The most fitted individual, after a given number of generations, represents the best candidate solution of the optimization problem, *i.e.* the number of K clusters that produce the best clustering structure. Algorithm **5.5.1** outlines the steps of the algorithm and in the next sections we describe each step in detail.

Algorithm 5.5.1 Genetic clustering algorithm (GCA) outline

  1: Initialize population
  2: Initialize mutation operator, selection operator and crossover operator.
  3: **while** Algorithm has not converged **do**
  4:     Evaluate fitness of population
  5:     Evolve population, resulting in a new population.
  6: **end while**

Population Initialization

The first step of the algorithm is to create and initialize a *population*. In this step, the algorithm will initialize the population with a number of individuals equal to the population size provided by the user. The size of individuals is randomly selected from the interval [2, K_{max}], where K_{max} is the upper bound of K, provided by the user. In terms of performance, it is not crucial to select an optimal upper bound value for K, because the evolution will resize the individuals to a value of K that results in a higher fitness level. However, the higher value of K_{max} may result in the creation of larger individuals, and consequently increase the time-complexity of the algorithm. The reason for introducing this upper bound is to inhibit the algorithm from creating unnecessary large individuals. For instance, it is rather rare to have data where its objects are so well-separated that the optimal K is close to the number of objects in the data set. The genes of each individual are randomly selected from the data set undergoing clustering. Note that we also check if individuals are valid, *i.e.* individuals cannot contain duplicates in their genetic material. Without this requirement individuals could represent invalid clustering structures.

The *chromosome* of an individual consists of K genes, where each gene represents a cluster centroid of size d (d is the number of dimensions of the data). Given a data set that contains two-dimensional data objects, $d = 2$ and $K = 3$, the chromosome of an individual would have the form:

$$\{(x_0, y_0), (x_1, y_1), (x_2, y_2)\}.$$

where each (x, y) represent the position of each cluster centroid in the search space. The search space constitutes the domain of the provided data set. Each individual represents a clustering structure, hence a candidate solution to the optimization problem, where an assigned fitness level determines how good the solution is.

Fitness Evaluation

Because individuals represent clustering structures, the fitness level is therefore based on validation of the clustering structure. Implementation of the different fitness evaluation methods from which the user may select are described in Section 5.5.6.

Evolve Population

After calculating the fitness level of individuals, the next step is to evolve the population to generate new individuals for the next generation. This process involves selection of parents, crossover and mutation. The user has to specify which operator to use for the various steps. First, the algorithm selects individuals for crossover by adding them to a collection of parents, known as the *mating pool*. The selection operator is applied to select individuals for the mating pool. The different selection operators the user may choose are described in Section 5.5.3. Next, the individuals of the mating pool are used as parents to create new individuals using the crossover operator. The various crossover operators are described in Section 5.5.5. The final step in the evolution of the population is to mutate individuals. All individuals, created by the crossover operator, are set up for mutation. Each of the K genes of an individual has the probability p_m of being mutated. The mutation operator is described in Section 5.5.4.

Termination Criteria

The algorithm runs for a number of generations provided by the user. The maximum number of generations depends on the size of the data to be analysed and the size of the population. Smaller populations may need a longer time to explore the search space, thus may rely on a high number of generations to converge. We have also introduced a termination criterion where the algorithm will terminate if the most fitted individual of the population does not improve across a given number of generations. Therefore, one could set a high number of maximum generations. The termination criteria will then stop the algorithm if it converges before the maximum number of generations is reached.

Time-Complexity

The time-complexity of the GCA is dependent on these operations:

- **Initialization of the population:** The time-complexity of this operation is dependent on the initial size of the population p, and the maximum size of individuals, K_{max}. The operation of checking if individuals contain duplicates has the time-complexity of $O(k^2 \cdot d)$, since we need to check if each gene is equal to any of the other genes. In the worst case, each of the p individuals are initialized with K_{max} genes. The initialization of the population will then have a time-complexity of $O(p \cdot k^2 \cdot d)$, where k is equal to K_{max}. Note that duplicates will be replaced by new data objects sampled from the data set, which means that we need to confirm the validity of the individual again. This continues until we have a valid individual. In worst case, where $K_{max} = n/2$, the time-complexity of this operation will move towards ∞. In most cases, the size of individuals are far from $n/2$, and since we are analysing data containing distinct data objects, we assume that the validity check will only be performed once for each gene.
- **Fitness evaluation:** The time-complexity of this operation depends on which fitness evaluation method one applies. The two implemented fitness evaluation methods, described in Section 5.5.6, have the same time-complexity of

$O(p \cdot n^2 \cdot d)$.

- **Evolving the population:**
  - ○ **Select individuals for crossover:** Time-complexity depends on which selection operator we employ and the size of the mating pool (worst case size is equal to p). For *Random selection* the time- complexity is equal to $O(p)$ and $O(p^3)$ for *Proportional selection*.
  - ○ **Crossover:** Using *Variable K Crossover*: $O(p \cdot n^2 \cdot d)$.
  - ○ **Mutation:** Using *Floating-point mutation*: $O(p \cdot n^3 \cdot d)$.

All the operations are performed sequentially once per generation t. The heaviest operation of the algorithm is the floating-point mutation operation, resulting in a time-complexity of $O(p \cdot n^3 \cdot d)$. This results in a **total time-complexity** of $O(t \cdot p \cdot n^3 \cdot d)$.

5.5.2. Differential Evolution Based Clustering Algorithm

In contrast to the genetic algorithm described in the previous section, a *Differential Evolution* algorithm will utilize information about the current population to evolve its individuals into more promising areas of the search space. This is achieved by generating mutation steps based on distances between individuals of the population. The crossover operator will produce an offspring by combining the mutated individual and its parent. In contrast to the genetic algorithm, crossover rate will determine how much the reproduced offspring is affected by the mutated individual.

The algorithms also differ in terms of the order the evolutionary operators are applied on the population. Using a genetic algorithm, one first uses the crossover operator on each individual of the population, producing a set of offsprings. The mutation operator is then applied to each offspring, where the mutated individuals constitute the evolved population surviving to the next generation. In contrast, an algorithm based on Differential Evolution will evolve each individual of the population separately, by first applying mutation and then use the mutated individual in the crossover operator to produce an offspring. The next sections will describe the implementation of a *Differential Evolution clustering algorithm* (DECA) that evolves individuals of variable chromosome size.

Population Initialization

To initialize the population of DECA, we use the same procedure as described for the GCA (in Section 5.5.1).

Mutation

As described in Section 3.7, for each individual $x_i(t)$ of the population the mutation operator creates a trial vector, $u_i(t)$, based on a target vector, $x_{i_1}(t)$, and two difference vectors, $x_{i_2}(t)$ and $x_{i_3}(t)$. Vectors are represented as individuals. The implemented mutation operator consists of two processes:

1. Selecting vectors for computing trial vector, $u_i(t)$.
2. Computing the trial vector as in Equation 3.17.

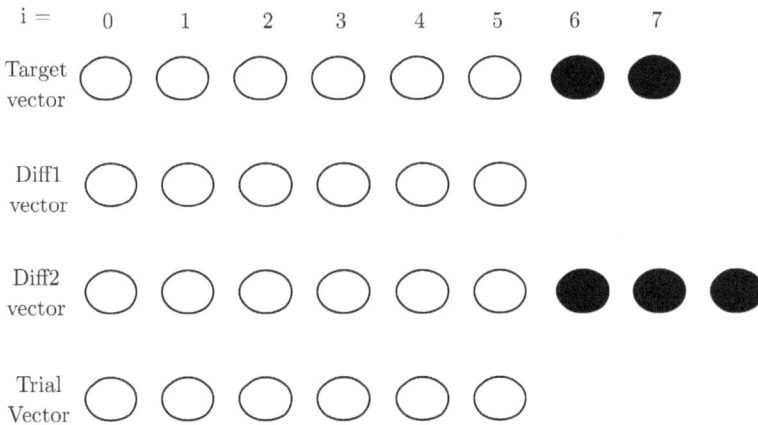

Fig. (5.4). Differential Evolution - creating a trial vector.

One needs to select individuals for the target vector and difference vectors where $x_i(t) \neq x_{i_1}(t) \neq x_{i_2}(t) \neq x_{i_3}(t)$. Either of the selection operators described in Section 5.5.3 can be used for vector selection. Computation of the trial vector is described in Algorithm **5.5.2**. Since it can be problematic to perform mathematical operations on vectors (represented by individuals) of different size, we need to adjust the vectors so that they are of equal size. This is done by setting the size of the resulting trial vector to be equal to the smallest of the selected individuals. When computing the trial vector, the algorithm ignores gene values of individuals that have a higher index than the size of the trial vector. This is illustrated in Fig. (**5.4**). The smallest individual is the *Diff1* vector of size 6, thus the size of the trial vector also equal to 6. The genes of index $i > 5$ of *Diff2* vector and *target* vector (filled with black in Fig. **5.4**) will be ignored when running Algorithm **5.5.2**, thus making it possible to create a trial vector when the selected individuals are of different size.

Algorithm 5.5.2 DE: Create trial vector

Require: Individual *targetvector, diff1, diff2* and scalingfactor β.

  1: Find minimum size *minSize* of the trial vector.

  2: Create a new Individual *scaledDiff* of size *minSize*.

  3: **for** index i, where $i < minSize$ **do** $\triangleright \beta(x_{i_2} - x_{i_3})$

  4:      ith gene of *scaledDiff* $\leftarrow \beta \times$ subtract(ith gene of *diff1*, ith gene of *diff2*) .

  5: **end for**

  6: Create new individual *trialvector* of size *minSize*.

  7: **for** index i, where $i < minSize$ **do** $\triangleright x_{i_1} + \beta(x_{i_2} - x_{i_3})$

  8:      ith gene of *trialvector* $\leftarrow$ sum(ith gene of *targetvector*, ith gene of *scaledDiff*).

  9: **end for**

10: **if** *trialvector* is *valid* **then**

11:      **Return** *trialvector*

12: **else**

13:      **Return** *targetvector*

14: **end if**

Only valid trial vectors are used in the crossover operator, *i.e.* the trial vector must fulfill requirements of partitional clustering. If not, the target vector is used as a trial vector of the crossover operator.

Crossover

Crossover is performed using an adapted version of the *Binomial Crossover* operator described in Section 3.7. A standard binomial crossover operator generates a set of crossover points J, randomly selected from n_x possible crossover points. n_x is the size of individuals undergoing crossover. The genes of the generated offspring are defined in Equation 3.18. Since we are working with individuals of different size we need to adapt the operator accordingly. The adapted binomial crossover operator is described in Section 5.5.5.

Termination Criteria

Similar to GCA, the DECA will either terminate after a maximum number of generations or when the algorithm has converged.

Time-complexity

The time-complexity of the differential algorithm is dependent on these components:

- **Initialization of the population:** The same time-complexity as for the GCA, $O(p \cdot k)$.
- **Evaluation of fitness:** In Section 5.5.6, $O(p \cdot n^2 \cdot d)$.
- **Evolution of the population:**
  Creating the trial vector: Four individuals may be selected by the operator, and if they are not distinct, new ones are selected. This goes on until we have a set of unique individuals. The implementation makes it hard to evaluate the time-complexity of this operation. The time-complexity of this operation is dependent on both size of and the diversity of the population. A low diversity will increase the probability of selecting equal individuals, thus increasing time-complexity of the operation. The same problem exists for smaller populations, where the probability of selecting the same individuals is high. Further analysis of the time-complexity assumes a $O(1)$ time-complexity for selecting four distinct individuals. As a result, creating the trial vector has the time-complexity of $O(k \cdot d)$, where k is the minimum size of difference vectors and d is the dimension of the data. The validity check has the time-complexity of Algorithm **5.4.1**, $O(n^2 \cdot d)$. Since the validity check is the heaviest operation, the resulting time-complexity of creating the trial vector is $O(p \cdot n^2 \cdot d)$.
  Crossover: By adopting the *Adapted Binomial crossover* (Section 5.5.2), the complexity is given by $O(p \cdot n^2 \cdot d)$.

Hence, the time-complexity of evolving the population is $O(p \cdot n^2 \cdot d)$.

The **total time-complexity** of the DECA is then $O(t \cdot p \cdot n^2 \cdot d)$, where t is the number of generations. This is based on the assumption that selecting individuals for the mutation operator is a constant-time operation.

5.5.3. Selection Operators

Random Selection

This operator will randomly select *n* copies of individuals from the population, meaning that each individual has a probability to be selected for the mating pool. The *time-complexity* of this operator is O(1), since selecting a random individual from the population using *Random.nextInt(populationSize)* is a constant-time operation.

Proportional Selection

Proportional selection operators are focused on selecting individuals with a high fitness level. Individuals are selected using the probability distribution proposed in [13] as

$$\rho(x_i(t)) = \frac{f_Y(x_i(t))}{\sum_{l=1}^{p} f_Y(x_l(t))} \qquad (5.1)$$

where $f_Y(x_i(t))$ denotes the normalized fitness level of x_i, and $\rho(x_i(t))$ denotes the probability of the individual $x_i(t)$ being selected. p denotes the size of the population.

For *maximization problems*, where higher fitness levels yield a better candidate solution, the normalized fitness level of individuals can be calculated using the following equation

$$f_Y(x_i(t)) = \frac{1}{1 + f_{max}(t) - f(x_i(t))} \qquad (5.2)$$

where $f_{max}(t)$ denotes the fitness level of the most fitted individual of generation t, and $f(x_i(t))$ denotes the fitness level of $x_i(t)$. The proportional selection operator is implemented as *Roulette Wheel Selection*, where the probability distribution of the population can be seen as a roulette wheel. Fig. (**5.5**) illustrates the roulette wheel selection, where individuals with a higher fitness level will be assigned a larger area of the roulette wheel, hence having a larger chance of being selected. The implementation of the proportional selection operator is described in Algorithm **5.5.3**.

The *time-complexity* of the proportional selection operator is dependent on the three processes:

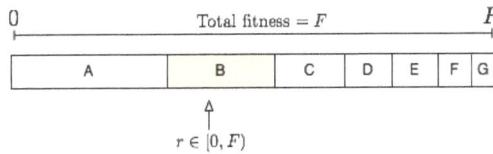

Fig. (5.5). Proportional Selection - Roulette Wheel Selection.

Algorithm 5.5.3 Selection operator: Proportional Selection

Require: Population *pop*

1: $i \leftarrow 0$
2: $sum \leftarrow \rho(x_i)$ where x_i is the ith individual of *pop*.   ▷ See Eq. 5.1.
3: $r \leftarrow$ random generated number.   ▷ from Uniform distribution $\in [0, 1)$
4: **while** $sum < r$ **do**
5:       $i \leftarrow i + 1$
6:       $sum \leftarrow sum + \rho(x_i)$
7: **end while**
8: **Return** selected individual: x_i.

- **Normalizing fitness level of individuals:** Using Equation 5.2, this operation has the time-complexity of $O(1)$.
- **Computing the selection probability for each individual:** When calculating the selection probability of an individual we first need to normalize its fitness level. The total time-complexity of this operation is of $O(p)$.
- **Selecting an individual (Equation 5.1):** The time-complexity of Algorithm **5.5.3** is dependent on the probability distribution of the individuals. In worst case, if r is close to 1 and the probability distribution of the population is such that when the while loop makes p steps, the time-complexity of selecting an individual from the population is $O(p^2)$. For each of the p steps of the while loop,

we compute the selection probability for all individuals.

The **total time-complexity** of the proportional selection is $O(p^2)$.

5.5.4. Mutation Operators

Floating-Point Mutation

We have implemented a version of *Floating-point mutation*, proposed in [26]. The implemented method differ from the proposed method in that each gene is set up for mutation. In the proposed method, the mutation operator will completely alter the genetic material of the individuals. By this approach we risk loosing the genetic material of good candidate solutions. By selecting each gene for mutation we reduce the chance of altering the fitted individuals completely. Each gene x_{ij}' is computed as:

$$x_{ij}' = \begin{cases} \pm 2 * \delta & \text{if } x_{ij} = 0.0, \\ \pm 2 * \delta * x_{ij} & \text{otherwise.} \end{cases} \qquad \textbf{(5.3)}$$

where x_{ij} denotes the *j*th gene of individual x_i, and δ is a random number in [0, 1]. The mutation rate p_m determines if the relative gene is going to be mutated. The reason for introducing the factor of 2 is to be able to generate negative mutation steps larger than the current gene value when mutating positive gene values (and the other way around) [26]. One can therefore never mutate gene values from a positive (negative) to a negative (positive) value. In the ± operator, + and − is each applied with a probability of 0.5. Since each gene is a DataObject, each attribute of the DataObject is mutated by Equation 5.3. Since the cluster centroids are sampled from the data set being clustered, one has to create new DataObjects during the mutation operation, to avoid altering the original data. If the mutation of a gene produces an invalid clustering structure, the mutation step is not valid and mutation is not performed. Invalid clustering structures and how to avoid them is discussed in Section 9.3. Algorithm **5.5.4** describes implementation of the Floating-point mutation operator.

Algorithm 5.5.4 Floating-point mutation

Require: Individual undergoing mutation and a random generation number δ.
1: **for all** *genes* of *individual* **do**
2:      $r \leftarrow$ random number sampled for the Uniform dist. of $[0, 1]$
3:      **if** $r \leq p_m$ **then**
4:          **for all** values of *DataObject* **do**
5:              Each value is mutated by Eq. 5.3
6:          **end for**
7:          **if** The mutated individual is *invalid* **then**   ▷ See Alg. 5.5.5
8:              The *gene* is not mutated.
9:          **end if**
10:     **end if**
11: **end for**

Algorithm 5.5.5 Floating-point mutation: check cluster validity

---

Require: individual *ind* of size K
1: *k-means* $\leftarrow$ K-Means algorithm with K clusters
2: **for all** genes i of *ind* **do**
3:     initialize the centroid of the ith cluster of *k-means* to ith gene of *ind*.
4: **end for**
5: Cluster data by employing algorithm 5.4.1.
6: **if** clustering structure has empty clusters **then**
7:     **return** false.
8: **else**
9:     **return** true.
10: **end if**

The time-complexity of mutating an individual is equal to $O(k \cdot d)$. This is because all k genes of an individual are set up for mutation, and each gene contains a data object of d dimensions. After a gene is mutated, we also need to perform the clustering, operation described in Algorithm **5.4.1**, in order to check if the mutation results in an invalid clustering structure. This operation has the time-complexity of $O(n^2 \cdot d)$ (see Section 5.4.2). Since $O(d) < O(n^2 \cdot d)$, the time-complexity of mutating an individual is $O(k \cdot n^2 \cdot d)$. In the worst case, $k = n/2$, which results in a time-complexity of $O(n^3 \cdot d)$. Since all p individuals of the population are set up for mutation, the **total time-complexity** of this operation is $O(p \cdot n^3 \cdot d)$.

5.5.5. Crossover Operators

Variable K Crossover

Variable K Crossover is a *sexual* crossover operator that performs one-point crossover (described in Section 3.3.1) when parents are of different size, proposed in [3]. Two parents are selected from the mating pool and set up for crossover. Selected parents will still be kept in the mating pool to mimic the ability of *well-adapted* individuals to reproduce more than once per generation. If they are able to reproduce, determined by the crossover rate p_c, two offsprings are created by performing one-point crossover on the two selected parents. Only valid offsprings are accepted (See Section 5.4), where invalid offsprings will be replaced by one of the parents. When working with individuals of different size, we need to create a separate crossover point for each parent within their respective boundaries. When we use a shared crossover point we risk that the point might be out of bounds for one of the parents. Only individuals of size $K \geq 2$ will be selected as parents for the operator, and as a result one can never create offsprings of size $K = 1$. There are various reasons why we apply this constraint:

- If the operator creates an individual of size $K = 1$, this individual would never be selected as parent for a later crossover operation. This means that the size of this individual would stay constant throughout the evolution and only explore the clustering structure in the domain of $K = 1$.
- After performing crossover, one could be left with a population where a large portion of its individuals are of size $K = 1$. The genetic material of these individuals will never be used for crossover. This drastically reduce the *diversity* in the population and limits the exploration possibilities of the algorithm.
- One rarely want to optimize clustering structures where the data can be grouped into one cluster.

The operation of creating an offspring is described in Algorithm **5.5.6**. The offsprings will replace the parents in the evolved population. This will continue until the number of requested individuals are created. Algorithm **5.5.7** presents pseudocode of the crossover operator.

Algorithm 5.5.6 Variable K Crossover: Create offspring

Require: Parents a and b, two crossover points c_1 and c_2.

1: $n \leftarrow c_1 +$ (size of $b - c_2$)   ▷ n is the size of the offspring.
2: $j \leftarrow c_2 + 1$ ▷ This is used to retrieve genes from the opposite parent.
3: **for all** i of n **do**
4:      **if** $i \leq c_1$ **then**
5:          The ith gene of *offspring* gets the value from the ith gene of parent a.
6:      **else**
7:          The ith gene of *offspring* gets the value from the jth gene of parent b
8:      **end if**
9: **end for**

The time-complexity of the Variable K Crossover operator is dependent on these operations:

- **Generating two crossover points, c_1 and c_2:** Both constant time operations, *i.e.* $O(1)$.
- **Creating offsprings:** The crossover operator creates two offsprings from two parents, where the total size of the offsprings is equal to the total size of the parents. Since the creation of the offspring consists of adding genetic material from parents, the time-complexity of the operator is dependent on the size of offsprings. In the worst case, the size of parents $k = n/2$ where n is equal to the number of data objects. This means that the total size of the offsprings is equal to n, thus the time-complexity of creating two offspring is equal to $O(n)$.

Algorithm 5.5.7 Variable K Crossover

Require: crossover rate p_c and two parents.

1: $r \leftarrow$ randomly generated number
2: **if** $r \leq p_c$ **then**
3:      Generate two crossover points, c_1 and c_2.
4:      Generate two offspring by applying Alg. 5.5.6 twice.
5:      **if** each offspring is valid **then**
6:          **Return** both of the generated offsprings.
7:      **else**
8:          **Return** invalid offspring(s) will be replaced by its parent(s).
9:      **end if**
10: **else**   ▷ Individuals will not reproduce.
11:      **Return** the two parents.
12: **end if**

- **Check if offsprings are valid:** The validity check consists of two operations:
  - Check if offsprings contain duplicate genes.
  - Check if the clustering structures of the offsprings contain empty clusters.

The operation of checking if offsprings contain duplicate genes has the time-complexity of $O(k^2 \cdot d)$. Checking if two centroids are equal, results in the time-complexity of $O(d)$. In the worst case, where $k = n/2$, the time-complexity of this operation is $O(n^2 \cdot d)$. To check if an offspring generates empty clusters, has the time-complexity of $O(n^2 \cdot d)$ since we need to cluster the data using the algorithm from Section **5.4.1**. This results in the time-complexity of $O(n^2 \cdot d)$.

The **total time-complexity** of the operator is then $O(n^2 \cdot d)$.

Adapted Binomial Crossover

In this section we describe the implementation of an *adapted binomial crossover operator* that is able to perform crossover on individuals of different size. A trivial solution would be to normalize the size of the parents, *i.e.* parent chromosomes are cropped so that both parents are of same size, and then perform regular binomial crossover.

An binomial crossover operator that handles variable chromosome lengths was proposed in [27], where the idea is that the genes of parents selected for crossover are divided into an equal number of segments. How many genes each segment contains is arbitrary, but it needs to contain at least one gene. The set of gene indices that constitute possible crossover points J, is replaced by a set of segment indices. With J replaced, crossover is carried out as described in Section 3.18. The purpose of dividing parents into segments is to enable the crossover operator to create individuals of arbitrary size, thus making the operator able to explore the entire search space. The outline of the adapted binomial crossover operator is described in Algorithm **5.5.8**.

Algorithm 5.5.8 Binomial crossover: variable chromosome size

Require: Individual *trial*, Individual *parent*
1: Find minimum number of segments.
2: Divide both *trial* and *parent* into segments.
3: Generate set of segments indices, J. ▷ randomly generated using Uniform
                                distribution.
4: **for** index $i <$ number of segments **do**
5:     **if** $i \in J$ **then**
6:        Add ith segment of Individual *trial* to offspring.
7:     **else**
8:        Add ith segment of Individual *parent* to offspring.
9:     **end if**
10: **end for**
11: **Return** offspring.

The operations that influence the time-complexity of the crossover operator are:

- **Dividing the genetic material of individuals into segments:** This is done on the individual x_i and the trial vector u_i. The genetic material of individuals is divided into segments by randomly selecting genes and adding them to a segment (selecting one gene has the time-complexity of $O(1)$). The time-complexity of the operation is dependent on the size of the individual, thus having the complexity of $O(k)$.

- **Generate the set of crossover points, J :** The size of J is randomly generated from the uniform distribution of $[0 \ldots k]$. The maximum number of segments is equal to k. This means that the operation of selecting a set of crossover points that is equal to the number of segments has the time-complexity of $O(k)$.

- **Selecting and adding genes from parents to form genes of offspring:** This operation consists of selecting segments of genes from either x_i or u_i. For each selected segment one has to add the genes of the segment to the offspring. The time-complexity of this operation is dependent on the size of the selected segment. In the worst case one could select the largest segments, where each one could have the size k. Since the number of segments can be equal to k, and each segment can have k genes, the time complexity of this operation is $O(k^2)$.

- **Check validity of the offspring:** The time-complexity of checking if an individual contains empty clusters is $O(n^2 \cdot d)$. To check if the genetic material of the offspring does not contain duplicates has the time-complexity of $O(n^2 \cdot d)$.

Checking if the offspring is valid is the heaviest operation, thus the **total time-complexity** is equal to $O(n^2 \cdot d)$.

5.5.6. Fitness Evaluation

Clustering Metric

Applying the objective function J, described in Equation 2.11, to evaluate the fitness of individuals, was proposed in [26], where the fitness of individual $x_i(t)$ is calculated as

$$F(x_i(t)) = \frac{1}{J}. \tag{5.4}$$

A minimization of the J value means that the *Euclidean distance* (See Equation 2.5) between the cluster centroids and the members of the corresponding clusters are small, implying compact clusters. The maximization of Equation 5.4 represents a high fitness level. Algorithm **5.5.9** describes the implementation of the fitness evaluation described above. The time-complexity of this operation is dependent on the following operations:

- **Adding cluster centroid to each of the k clusters:** Adding centroid to a cluster is an $O(1)$ operation, and since this is done for all k clusters, the time-complexity is $O(k)$.
- **Clustering of the data and updating centroids:** From Section 5.4.2, the time-complexity of these operations is $O(n^2 \cdot d)$ and $O(n \cdot d)$.
- **Calculation of the clustering metric J:** To calculate the clustering metric, we add the clustering metric of each cluster together. To calculate the clustering metric of one cluster, we measure the distance between the centroid and all members of the corresponding cluster. Calculating the Euclidean distance between two data objects has the time-complexity of $O(d)$. This is done for all k clusters and results in a total time-complexity of $O(k \cdot n \cdot d)$, where n is the number of patterns assigned to each cluster.
- **Adding updated centroids to individuals:** The time-complexity of this

operation is dependent on the number of k, thus $O(k)$.

Algorithm 5.5.9 Fitness evaluation

Require: list of individuals in the population *pop*
  1: **for all** individuals i in population *pop* **do**
  2:     Initialize clustering algorithm *K-Means*
  3:     **for all** genes of i **do**
  4:        Set clustering centroids of *K-Means* to be equal to the genes of i
  5:     **end for**
  6:     Cluster the data
  7:     Update centroids
  8:     Compute J-value, define in Equation 2.11.
  9:     Set fitness of i to be equal to $1/J$
10: **end for**

Since the heaviest task is the clustering of the data, the **total time-complexity** of evaluating the fitness of an individual is $O(n^2 \cdot d)$.

Davies-Bouldin Index

While the *clustering metric* only focuses on intracluster distances to validate clustering structures, *Davies-Bouldin Index (DBI)* (described in section 2.1.6) includes *intercluster* distances when evaluating clustering structures. As before, since individuals represent K cluster centroids, one evaluates the fitness of individuals by clustering the data using the K-means algorithm. DBI evaluates clustering structures by measuring how *compact* and *well-separated* the clusters are. To do this, one is dependent on the *minimum distance* between clusters (see Equation 2.17), and the *maximum distance* between members of a cluster (see Equation 2.18). The pseudocode of these two operations is described in Algorithm **5.5.10** and Algorithm **5.5.11**.

Calculating the minimum distance between two clusters is dependent on the number of members of each cluster. In worst case, each cluster could have n/2 members where n is the number of data objects undergoing clustering. Calculating the distance between two objects has the time-complexity of $O(d)$. This means that the time-complexity of Algorithm **5.5.10** is $O(n^2 \cdot d)$. Algorithm **5.5.11** also has the time-complexity of $O(n^2 \cdot d)$ since to compute the maximum inter-cluster distance, one needs to calculate the Euclidean distance ($O(d)$) between all members of a cluster.

To be able to evaluate the DBI of a clustering structure we need, for each cluster C_i, to find the cluster C_j (where $i \neq j$) that yields the largest intra-cluster distance and smallest inter-cluster distance. For all k clusters, this yields the time-complexity of $O(k^2 \cdot n^2 \cdot d)$. In worst case, the size of $k = $ n/2. In this scenario, each cluster have two members, and to calculate the maximum intra-cluster distance and minimum inter-cluster distance becomes constant-time operation. This implies that the **total time-complexity** of the Davies-Bouldin Index is equal to $O(n^2 \cdot d)$.

Algorithm 5.5.10 Davies-Bouldin index: minimum distance between two clusters

---

Require: Two clusters, C_1 and C_2
 1: *minDistance* ← minimum distance found.
 2: **for** each member x of C_1 **do**
 3:     **for** each member x of C_2 **do**
 4:         Calculate *distance* between C_1 and C ▷ based on Euclidean
                                                                        Distance (Eq. 2.5)
 5:         **if** *distance* < *minDistance* **then**
 6:             *minDistance* ← *distance*
 7:         **end if**
 8:     **end for**
 9: **end for**
10: **Return** the minimum distance found.

By applying these methods to the Davies-Bouldin Index, defined in Equation. 2.20, the fitness of individual x_i is calculated as

$$\frac{1}{DBI_i} \tag{5.5}$$

Algorithm 5.5.11 Davies-Bouldin index: maximum intracluster distance

---

Require: A cluster, C_1.

1: $maxDistance \leftarrow$ maximum distance found.
2: **for** each member x_i of C_1 **do**
3:     **for** each member x_j of C_1 where $x_i \neq x_j$ **do**
4:         Calculate *distance* between x_i and x_j. ▷ based on Euclidean Distance (Eq. 2.5)
5:         **if** *distance* > *maxDistance* **then**
6:             $maxDistance \leftarrow distance$
7:         **end if**
8:     **end for**
9: **end for**
10: **Return** the maximum distance found.

Higher inter-cluster distances and smaller intra-cluster distances yield a higher fitness level.

CHAPTER 6

Data Visualization

Abstract: Different methods for visualization of data are described in the chapter. One important aspect is how to handle colours. Colour are separated in three different sub-channels. Different methods to reduce the dimension of data are also described.

Keywords: Data types, Dissimilarity matrix, Multi-dimensional scaling, Normalization, Principal components, Visual channels.

6.1. INTRODUCTION

In computer science visualization is defined as the visual representation of a domain using graphics, images or animation, to present the data or the structures of large data sets [28]. Visualization is used to understand the meaning of data, in situations where the problem may be too vague for a computer to handle [29]. For instance, illustrating the benefits of visualisation, is a subway map. The purpose of a subway map is to illustrate a subway system, consisting of subway lines, stations and transit points. This makes it easier for travellers to find the best way to travel from location A to location B. We may imagine what kind of problems a traveller needs to cope with if presented by only the raw data, containing for instance, the GPS-coordinates of each subway station. Visualization provides us with two types of information [28]:

1. Answers to concrete questions and hypothesis related to a given data set.
2. Facts about data of a given data set that one is unaware of.

Visualization may be used to answer both *quantitative* and *qualitative* questions. For quantitative questions, *e.g. "what is the output of function f(x) for all values of x within a given interval?"*. Visualization is not indispensable, it is an intuitive way to represent intervals rather than displaying a list of values. But for qualitative questions, visualization is indispensable. An example of a qualitative question is *"given a medical scan of a patient, are there any anomalies that indicate medical problems?"*. A computer program could find patterns in a blood sample that differ from other patterns, but it is not able to classify it as an anomaly [28]. One needs a human expert, for instance a doctor, to analyse the pattern. His opinion is based on prior expertise and experience. However, human experts are not able to make good decisions without being presented with meaningful data. Thus, advocating the importance of using visualization.

6.2. DATA TYPES

In cluster analysis the data type determines which operations one may utilize when analysing the data. In visualization, the data types define boundaries on how one may visualize the data. If the purpose is to visualize spatial data, one may choose an approach where the spatial information is emphasized and not lost. T. Munzer defines three types of data [29]: *quantitative, ordered and categorical data*. Quantitative data is often numerical. We can use arithmetic operations on them. One cannot do arithmetical operations on ordered data, but they have a well-defined ordering that one can utilize. Categorical data has no ordering. The data may only be divided into groups. In some data sets there exists a specific relationship between its members, and it is important that the visualization scheme expresses these relationships. This is referred to as *relational data* or *graphs* [29]. Some visualization guidelines of certain types of data are illustrated in section 6.3.

6.3. VISUAL CHANNELS

Visual channels are used to encode information [29]. Examples of visual channels are spatial information, such as horizontal and vertical positions, color, size *and shape*. Multiple visual channels are applied to represent the different dimensions of some *d*-dimensional data object. Visualizing a 3-dimensional vector, $x = \{x_1, x_2, x_3\}$, in a scatter plot one could use vertical and horizontal spatial points to represent values of x_1 and x_2, and size of the plotted points to represent values for x_3. When selecting the type of a visual channel to represent some data, it is important to consider the characteristics of the visual channels [29]. Not all channels are equally *distinguishable*, and studies have shown that people's ability to distinguish information encoded in different visual channels from each other, is dependent on the *data type* one is using. Some visual channels work well for categorical data, but not for ordered data, where the order of objects needs to be emphasized. *Separability* is an important characteristic of a visual channel. When visualizing categorical data it is important that the user can separate two categories from each other. The positioning of different objects is highly separable, but distinguishing objects by their vertical and horizontal size may be difficult [29]. Color is a powerful channel, but to avoid confusing the viewer, one has to consider its properties before applying it to a visualization problem [29]. Color may be separated into three different sub-channels:

- *Hue*
- *Saturation*
- *Lightness*

All available colors are derivatives of the primary colors red, green and blue (RGB), and the *hue* represents a given combination of these three colors. The different values of hue are represented in Fig. (**6.1a**) (image obtained from [30]). *Saturation* defines how intense a color is, from a slight grey tone to a vivid color, illustrated in Fig. (**6.1b**) (image obtained from [31]). *Lightness* defines how light/dark the relative color is. The three sub-channels in combination are illustrated in Fig. (**6.1c**) (image obtained from [32]).

Hue is good for visualizing categorical data because one could generate a large set of hues that are separable from each other [29]. But it is not appropriate when representing ordered data because it does not have any implicit perceptual ordering [29]. For instance, it is impossible to order yellow, purple and pink. For ordered data, it would be more preferable to use lightness or saturation because of its implicit ordering. The number of channels to use for spatial layouts has been extensively discussed [29]. Compared to 2D visualization, three dimensions makes an additional perspective when visualizing data objects.

However, researchers have begun to experience the *cost* of 3-dimensional visualization of datasets. The costs are referred to as *Occlusion* and *Perspective distortion*. Occlusion is when some data objects of a data set are hidden behind other data objects, from a certain viewpoint [29]. This makes it challenging for users to understand the structure of the data set. This is not a problem when the user is familiar with the data set, and has a mental map of its structure. However, it becomes challenging when visualizing unfamiliar data, where the user has no expectations of its structure [29]. Based on past experience, an individual may be able to judge heights on familiar objects, even if object far away may appear smaller.

(a) Hue

(b) Saturation

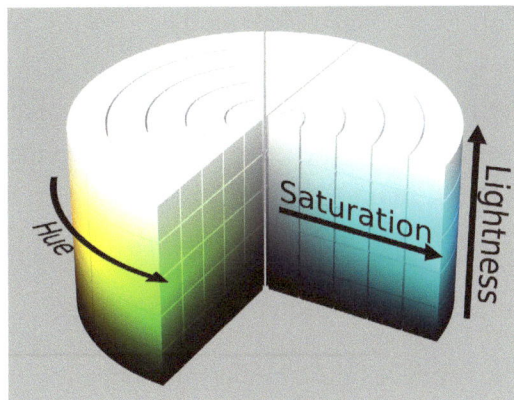

(c) HSL model

Fig. (6.1). Color channels.

This is due to the perspective distortion [29]. Perspective distortion is the phenomena where objects of the same size appear to be of different size, since one is closer than the other.

As a result, comparing heights in a 3-dimensional bar chart is more difficult than in a 2-dimensional chart, because the latter consists of horizontal aligned bars. In a 3-dimensional chart the bars are not only of different size, but some bars are closer to the viewer than others, making it difficult to judge their size.

6.4. HIGH-DIMENSIONAL DATA

High dimensional data makes visualization complex. By adding color and size, one can probably visualize data objects of five dimensions within a regular 3D scatter plot. However, more dimensions may make the visualization cluttered and less intuitive. To solve this problem many methods for *dimension reduction* have been proposed. Dimension reduction is the process of mapping some input data from a high-dimensional space, $\mathbb{R}^d$, to a space, $\mathbb{R}^{d'}$, of a dimension where d > d' [6].

$$F(x) : \mathbb{R}^d \to \mathbb{R}^{d'} \qquad \textbf{(6.1)}$$

Dimension reduction is possible because some features of data objects are a result of subjective measurements, and do not add any fundamental structural information to the data objects. They could be discarded without loosing any structural information about the data. In addition, one could also find more interesting hidden structures in the data represented by a lower dimension. The goal of reducing the dimension is to find the smallest subset of features necessary to illustrate the main structures or variance in a dataset. A proposed method is *Classical Multi-Dimensional Scaling (CMDS)* [33].

6.4.1. Classical Multi-Dimensional Scaling

This method reduces the number of dimensions in the data based on the idea that the most interesting information, in terms of comparing data objects, can be found in the dimensions with the largest variance. By performing *AMDS*, we transform data objects from a *d*-dimensional space to a d'-dimensional space, where d > d', while retaining as much of the variation in the data as possible [33]. The variation in the data is represented by *principal components*.

For instance, there exist d principal components for data in a d-dimensional space. When transforming data objects from $R^d \rightarrow R^{d'}$, only the d' principal components that represent the largest variation in the data are relevant. Basically, we use CMDS to create a representation of the data in terms of their principal components, thus presenting the data objects in terms of their most interesting features. The new representation is presented in a coordinate matrix X defined as

$$X_{n,d} = \begin{pmatrix} X_{1,1} & \cdots & X_{1,d} \\ X_{2,1} & \cdots & X_{2,d} \\ \vdots & \ddots & \vdots \\ X_{n,1} & \cdots & X_{n,d} \end{pmatrix} \tag{6.2}$$

where $X_{n,d}$ denotes the coordinates of the nth data object, and d denotes the number of principal components. In the next paragraphs we give a short introduction to the different steps of CMDS. A more detailed explanation is given in [33].

To understand the different steps of CMDS we need to introduce some theory of *eigenvectors* and *eigenvalues*. Given the equation

$$Ax = \lambda x \tag{6.3}$$

the non-zero vector x is an *eigenvector*, if when multiplied with the *squared matrix A* ($n \times n$), it becomes a scaled version of itself, moving in the same or opposite direction. The scaling factor (or multiplier), denoted by λ, is called the *eigenvalue*. Eigenvectors and eigenvalues exist in pairs. A principal component is the eigenvector with the highest eigenvalue, *i.e.* the direction of the largest variation of the data.

CMDS produce the coordinate matrix X by performing eigenvalue decomposition on the scalar product matrix $B_\Delta = XX'$, a process that consists of four steps [33]:

1. **Compute dissimilarity matrix Δ:**

Given n data objects, a dissimilarity matrix Δ is a $n \times n$ matrix defined as

$$
\Delta_{n,n} = \begin{pmatrix} D_{1,1} & D_{1,2} & \cdots & D_{1,n} \\ D_{2,1} & D_{2,2} & \cdots & D_{2,n} \\ \vdots & \vdots & \ddots & \vdots \\ D_{n,1} & D_{n,2} & \cdots & D_{n,n} \end{pmatrix}
\tag{6.4}
$$

where $D_{i,j}$ denotes the *Euclidean distance* (Eq. 2.5) between the ith and the jth data object for all $i, j \in N$.

2. **Apply *double centring* (Eq. 6.5) to Δ, producing the scalar product matrix B_Δ:**

B_Δ is defined as

$$
B_\Delta = -\frac{1}{2}J\Delta J
\tag{6.5}
$$

where J is defined as

$$
J = I - n^{-1}11'
\tag{6.6}
$$

where I denotes the *identity matrix* and 1 denotes the column matrix of 1's. $1'$ denotes the transpose of matrix 1 and n^{-1} denotes the inverse of the vector n.

3. **Compute eigenvalue decomposition of B_Δ:**

$$
B_\Delta = Q\Lambda Q'
\tag{6.7}
$$

where Q is a $n \times d$ matrix representing d eigenvectors, and Λ is an $d \times d$ matrix representing d eigenvalues corresponding to eigenvectors.

4. **Compute coordinate matrix X:**

The coordinate matrix X is derived from the multiplication of the d eigen-vectors and their corresponding eigenvalues, where the d eigenvectors representing the largest variance in the data, *i.e.* the ones with the highest corresponding eigenvalues. Based on Q and Λ from step 3, X is defined as

$$X = Q\Lambda^{1/2} \tag{6.8}$$

where $\Lambda^{1/2}$ denotes the square root of matrix Λ, *i.e.* the square-root of each element of Λ. As before, these d eigenvectors represent the largest variation in the data set.

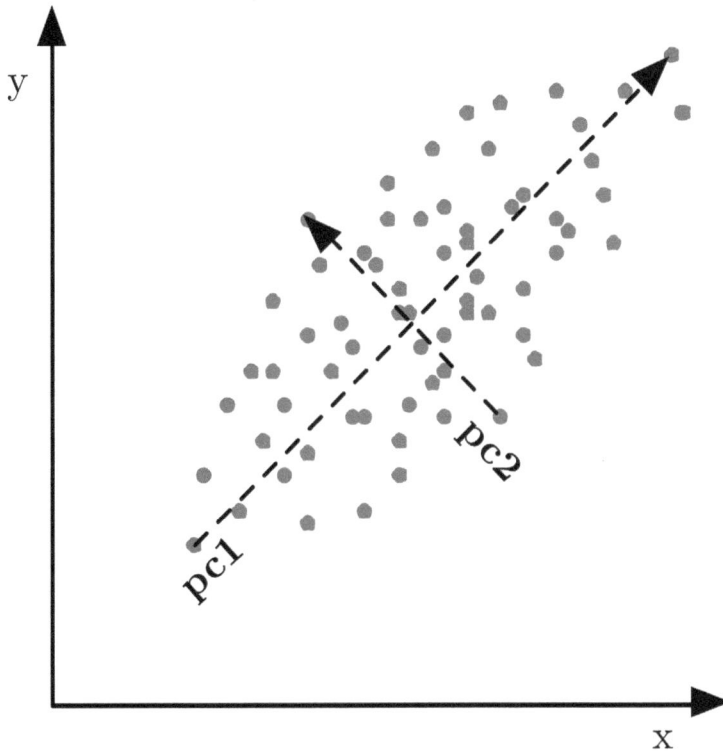

Fig. (6.2). CMDS - two principal components.

Fig. (**6.2**) illustrates an example of a two-dimensional scatter plot that contains arbitrary *two*-dimensional data objects and two corresponding principal components. Note that we could visualize the data presented in the example without the need to perform dimension reduction, if there are only two dimensions in the data. The eigenvector that represents the highest variance in the data set is denoted as *pc*1. The eigenvector that represents the second highest variance is denoted as *pc*2. After performing CMDS on the data objects we can use the coordinates from the resulting coordinate matrix X to plot the data in a two-dimensional scatter plot, in terms of the two principal coordinates, *pc*1, *pc*2, illustrated in Fig. (**6.3**). Instead of using x and y as axis the two principal components are used.

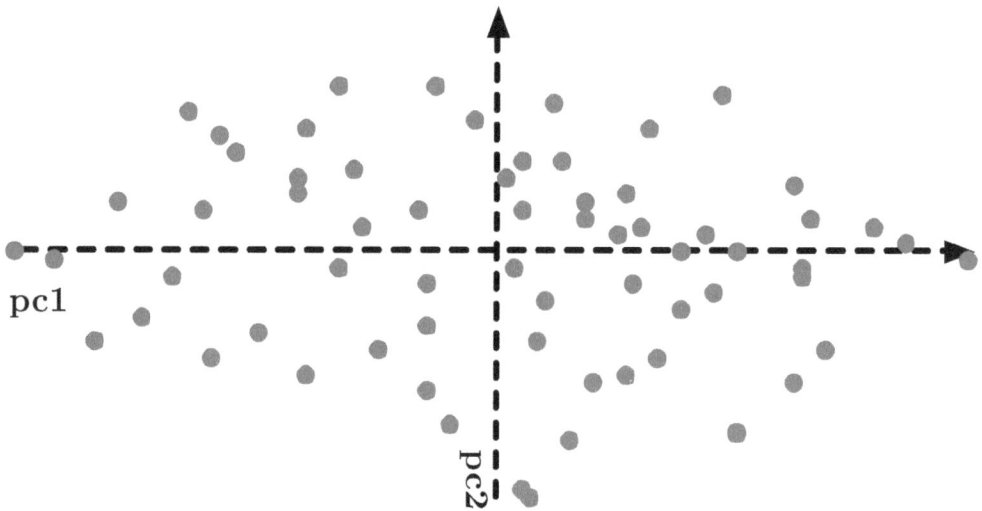

Fig. (6.3). CMDS - visualising data using principal components.

Another common application of the CMDS is to reduce first the dimensionality of the data, and then perform clustering in the reduced space [7]. In our system we are using the CMDS to transform data from a d-dimensional space to a two-dimensional space, $R^d \rightarrow R^2$, to be able to visualize the results of cluster analysis in a two-dimensional scatter plot.

6.5. IMPLEMENTATION

The visualization of the resulting clustering structure provided by the evolutionary clustering algorithms from Section 5.5, is dependent on four sequential operations, depicted in Algorithm **6.5.1**. Further more, this section will describe the implementation of these four operations and their respective time-complexity.

Algorithm 6.5.1 The steps of visualization

Require: A clustering structure, K.
  1: Normalize all data objects of the clustering structure K.
  2: Generate a dissimilarity matrix of data objects in the clustering structure K.
  3: Reduce number of dimensions using CMDS   ▷ Section 6.4.
  4: Plot data in a two-dimensional scatter chart.

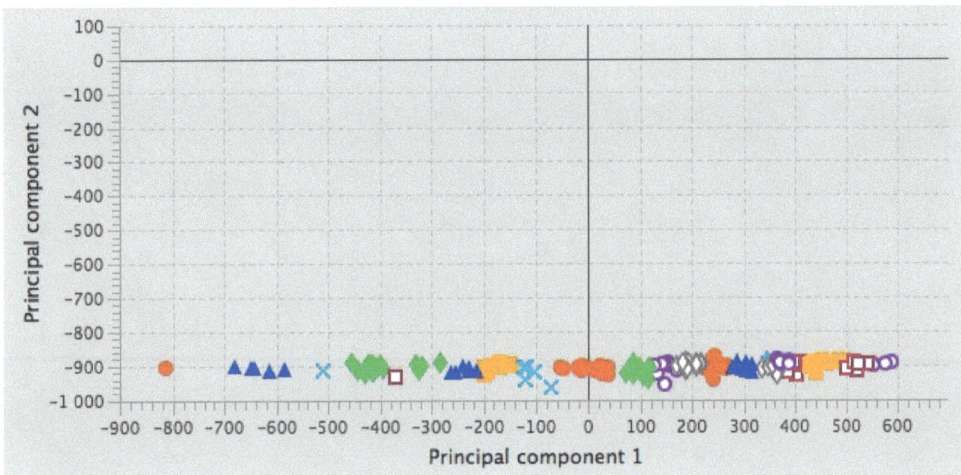

Fig. (6.4). CMDS with non-normalized data.

Step 1: Normalization

Before we perform CMDS we may need to normalize the data, since each dimension of data objects usually represents independent features, and are most likely measured using different numerical units. Fig. (**6.4**) shows the results of CMDS where the data has not been normalized. The data is plotted in terms of the two principal components, where *principal component 1* represents the dimension that produces the largest variance, and *principal component 2* represents the dimension containing the second largest variance in the data. The variation represented by *principal component 1* is much larger than the variance presented by *principal component 2*. Therefore, the impact of the second largest variance is lost in the visualization. As a result, we only see how the data objects differ in terms of *principal component 1*. By visualizing clustering structures, it is hard to get any useful information when the data is only displayed using the first principal component. The situation is illustrated in Figs. (**6.4** and **6.5**) visualizes the same data, but now the data is normalized using *min-max normalization* (see Section 2.1.3). By using min-max normalization the variance will be represented in the same range of [0, 1]. As a result we are able to show the data objects in terms of both the principal components.

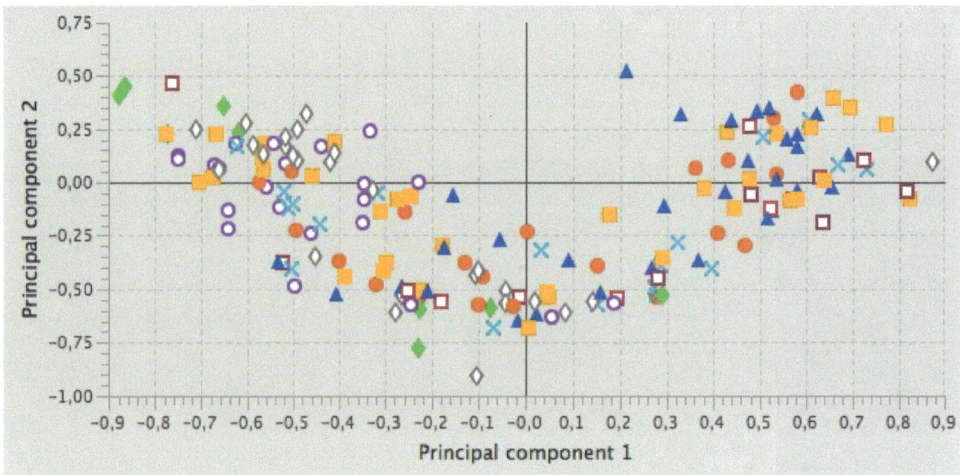

Fig. (6.5). CMDS with normalized data.

Step 2: Generate Dissimilarity Matrix

Since the cluster analysis is performed before we reduce the dimensional of the data, it is important that the clustering information is preserved during the dimension reduction. It is hard to store any clustering information in the data objects since they are represented as vectors and transformed using CMDS. We have implemented a mechanism where the n data objects are added to a list where the ordering is based on cluster membership, meaning that the first n data objects are member of cluster no. 1, the next n objects are member of cluster no. 2, and so on. Consequently, this list is employed when generating the dissimilarity matrix Δ, described in algorithm **6.5.2**. assuming that the ordering of the n data objects is preserved during the dimension reduction. The labelling of data objects (in step 4) will now be correct. The time-complexity of Algorithm **6.5.2** is $O(n^2 \cdot d)$.

Step 3: Dimension Reduction Using CMDS

To reduce the number of dimensions we perform CMDS using the Java library *MDSJ* [34], a free Java library for multi-dimensional scaling. MDSJ will perform CMDS by taking the dissimilarity matrix generated in the previous step, and produce the two-dimensional coordinate matrix X. It is difficult to calculate the computational complexity of producing the coordinates matrix X since we are using the MDSJ library. However, a standard implementation of CMDS has time-complexity of $O(n^3)$, where n are the number of data objects [35].

Algorithm 6.5.2 Generate dissimilarity matrix

Require: A list of the n data objects, ordered in terms of cluster membership.
1: Create a $n \times n$ dissimilarity matrix, A.
2: index $i \leftarrow 0$
3: index $j \leftarrow 0$
4: **for** $i \rightarrow n$ **do**
5:     **for** $j \rightarrow n$ **do**
6:         $dist \leftarrow$ *Euclidean distance* (Alg. 2.5) from the ith data object to the jth
                                    data object.
7:         $A[i, j] \leftarrow dist.$
8:     **end for**
9: **end for**
10: **return** dissimilarity matrix A.

Step 4: Plotting of Data

The system visualizes the clustering structures by plotting the coordinates provided by the coordinate matrix X in the previous step, in a two-dimensional scatter plot. The scatter plot is created using an instance of *ScatterChart*-class of JavaFX. Members of a cluster are added to the same *series* (Object of JavaFX), and each series is provided to the *ScatterChart*. The purpose of assigning the data objects to different series is to be able to assign each cluster with a distinct label in the scatter plot. This operation is outlined in Algorithm **6.5.3** and has a time-complexity of $O(n)$, where n are the number of data objects. JavaFX is described in Section 7.6.

Algorithm 6.5.3 Adding data objects to series

Require: Coordinate matrix X, where data objects are ordered in terms of cluster membership.

  1: Create a $n \times n$ dissimilarity matrix, A.
  2: index $i \leftarrow 0$
  3: index $j \leftarrow 0$
  4: **for** $i < K$, where K is the number of clusters **do**
  5:      Create a new series.
  6:      **for** $j < n$, where n is the number of cluster members **do**
  7:          Add coordinates of row i of X to the series.
  8:      **end for**
  9: **end for**

CHAPTER 7

User Interface

Abstract: The chapter gives an introduction to the architecture based on Model-View - Controller (MVC) patterns. Such an architecture separates the user interface from the business logic. The MVC enables us to divide the system into three components. The user provides the parameter values. When an algorithm is terminated the results may be shown graphically.

Keywords: Evolutionary operators, JavaFX, MVC.

7.1. INTRODUCTION

This chapter gives an overview of the *User Interface* (UI) of the system. The UI facilitates the interaction between the user and the system and provides the following functionality:

1. **Import data to the system**
2. **Select/initialize evolutionary clustering algorithms**
3. **Select/initialize evolutionary operators**
4. **Visualize the clustering structure**

The different functionality will be described in Sections 7.3, 7.4, 7.5 and 7.6. As mentioned in Section 5.2, the architecture of the system complies to the MVC pattern which separates the UI from the business logic. The MVC pattern and its role in the system is presented in Section 7.2.

7.2. MODEL-VIEW-CONTROLLER

The *Model-View-Controller* enables us to divide the system into three different subsystems: *Model, View and Controller* [36]. By doing this we separate the

Terje Kristensen

business logic (the model) from the UI (the view), and as a result, modification in either subsystem will not affect the other. All communication between the two is performed using the controller subsystem. By employing JavaFX to develop the UI we enforce the MVC pattern on our system. The user interface is created by defining the different UI components using a XML-based language known as FXML. The behaviour of the different components is defined in a separate controller class. Fig. (**7.1**) illustrates a basic example of how the MVC pattern is employed in the system. All UI components are defined in the *UI* FXML document, where the specific behaviour of each component is defined in *UIController*. The model, *i.e.* business logic in this example, are the classes marked with blue. For instance, the user decides to use the DECA to perform the cluster analysis, and specifies this through the *UI* (See Section 7.4). The *UIController* then creates an instance of the selected algorithm and run the algorithm on behalf of the *UI*. The algorithm analyses the data and provides the *UIController* with the results from the analysis. The *UIController* may alter relevant *UI* components based on the results from the analysis.

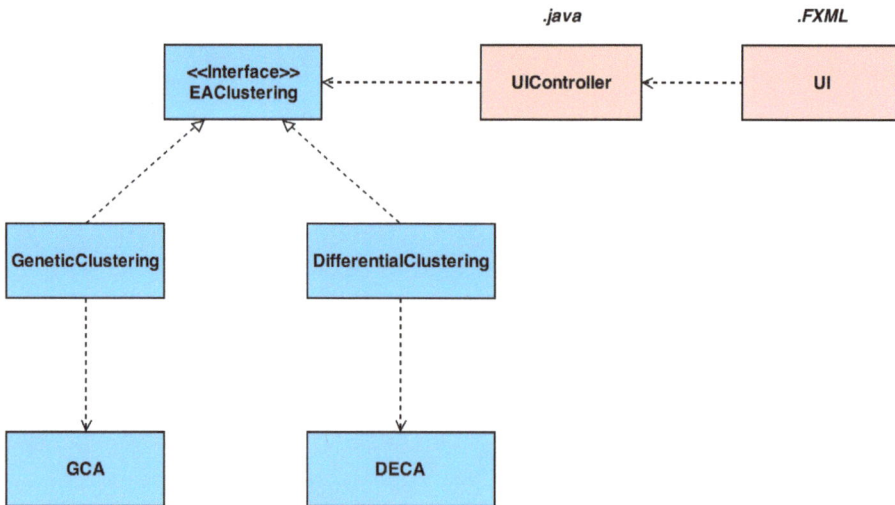

Fig. (7.1). Model-View-Controller using JavaFX.

7.3. IMPORT OF DATA

Fig. (**7.2**) shows the functionality that enables the user to upload data to the system. The user specifies *from/to* indices that the DataReader employs to create

DataObjects (see Section 5.4.1), represented by the *"From index:"* and *"To index:"* input fields in the figure.

Fig. (7.2). Import of data.

When pressing the "import data"-button, a pop-up window lets the user browse the file system to locate the specific data set that the user wants to analyse (see Fig. **7.3**). Note that the indices must be specified before importing the data.

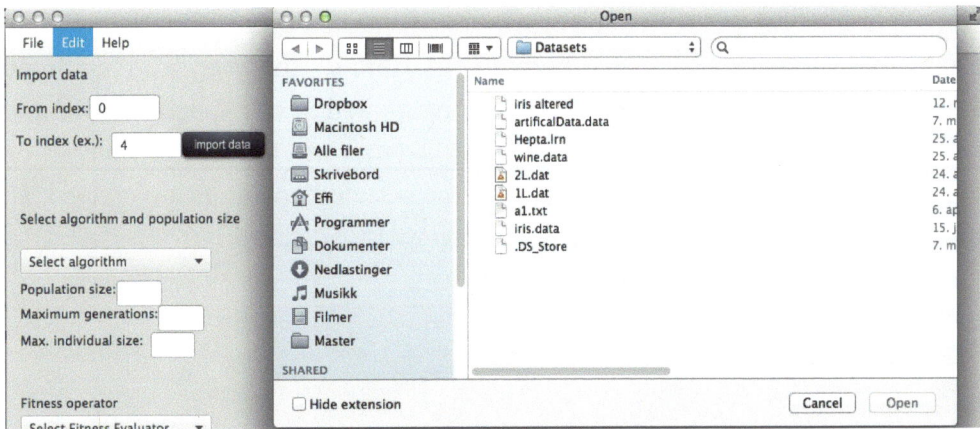

Fig. (7.3). Browsing the file system.

7.4. SELECTING AND INITIALIZING THE ALGORITHMS

From the drop-down menu in Fig. (**7.4**), the user may select which of the different ECAs from Section 5.5 to be used in the cluster analysis. The user must also provide parameter values, such as *population size, maximum number of generations and the maximum size of individuals.*

After providing the parameters, the user must press the "save"-button to create an instance of the selected algorithm (with the specified parameters).

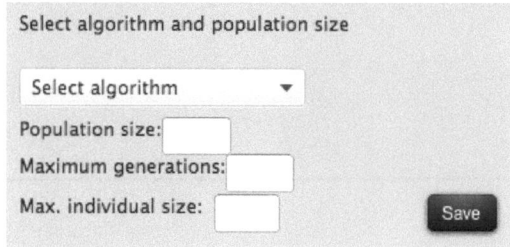

Fig. (7.4). Selecting and initializing algorithm.

7.5. SELECTING AND INITIALIZING EVOLUTIONARY OPERATORS

The functionality is presented in the screenshot given in Fig. (**7.5**) helps the user in selecting and initializing evolutionary operators for evolving the population. Note that *elitism* and selection of mutation operator only is available for the GCA, since the DECA does not employ these features (mutation in the DECA is described in Section 5.5.2). All the crossover operators described in Section 5.5.5 are available and may be selected by both algorithms. However, we recommend that the Variable K Crossover operator is only applied in GCA, and the Binomial Crossover operator is only applied in DECA. To perform the cluster analysis one press the "cluster data"-button. Instances of the selected operators are created, and the actual algorithm is being executed on the imported data.

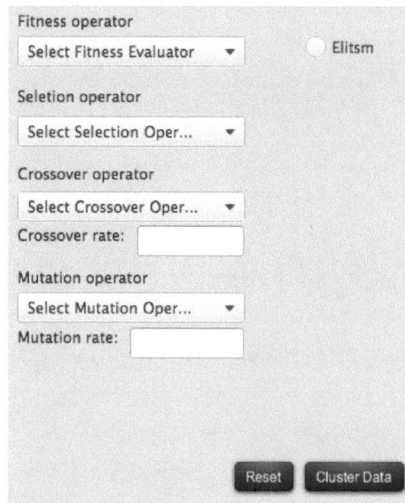

Fig. (7.5). Selecting and initializing evolutionary operators.

7.6. VISUALIZATION

When the algorithm has terminated, the result will be presented using a line chart and a scatter plot. An example of a trial run of the GCA using a arbitrary data set is given in Fig. (**7.6**). The line chart on the top of the figure illustrates the size of the most fitted individual found in each generation, where the *X*- axis depicts the generation number and the *Y*-axis depicts the size of the most fitted individuals. The plot beneath the line chart gives a two-dimensional representation of the best clustering structure found by using ECA. The preprocessing and plotting of the data were described in Section 6.5. In this example, we see that the optimal clustering structure contains two clusters.

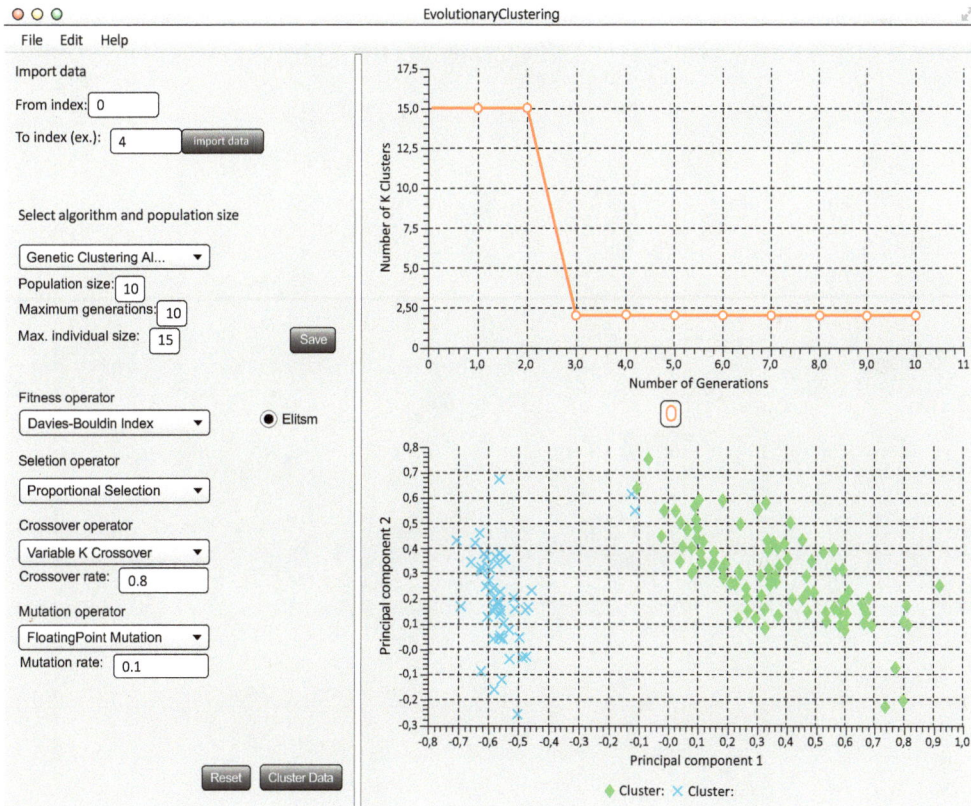

Fig. (7.6). An overview of the user interface.

The members of each clusters have been assigned different labels (labels are assigned beneath the scatter chart). We also mentioned in Section 6.5 that the members of each cluster were assigned a distinct label to make it easier to visualize. The scatter plot is created using an instance of the *Scatter-Chart* class of JavaFX. One limitation by using this class is that it only provides eight different labels. When visualizing more than eight series of data (series represents clusters in our case), previous applied labels are used. Different clusters may be assigned to the same labels, and as a result it can be difficult to distinguish the different clusters of the scatter plot.

CHAPTER 8

A Case Study

Abstract: To compare the different algorithms three data sets have been used. Different benchmarking sets have been applied and the results of the experiments are presented in tables and illustrated graphically.

Keywords: DECA, GCA, Hepta, Iris and Wine, JavaFX, Median, Scatter Chart.

8.1. INTRODUCTION

The purpose of the case study is to compare the performance of the evolutionary clustering algorithms presented in Section 5.5 by using some *benchmarking criteria*. We want to explore if the algorithms are able to classify the correct number of clusters when presented with data of different complexity. In addition, we want to compare the quality of the solutions provided by the algorithms.

8.2. BENCHMARKING ENVIRONMENT AND CRITERIA

To perform benchmark comparisons of the different algorithms we use three data sets:

- **Hepta** – artificial data created for benchmarking purposes of the clustering algorithms.
- **Iris** – three species of the Iris flower.
- **Wine** – wines from three different cultivars from the same region in Italy.

The three data sets differ in size, both the number of data objects and the dimension of the data, and also how hard it is to classify the clusters. Some data sets contain clusters that overlap, meaning that the clusters are hard to separate.

This makes it harder to determine the correct number of clusters. The characteristics of the different data sets are described in Section 8.3.1, 8.3.2 and 8.3.3, respectively.

When we compare heuristic optimization algorithms, we need to run the algorithms more than once to remove the randomness from the benchmarking results. In the test environment, each algorithm is run r independent *trial runs* for each data set.

8.2.1. Benchmarking Criteria

The benchmarking criteria we have used are:

- **Average fitness of solutions**
  The average quality, $Q_{average}$, of the candidate solutions obtained from the trial runs is calculated as

$$Q_{average} = \frac{1}{r}\sum_{i=0}^{r} F_i(x) \tag{8.1}$$

  where $F_i(x)$ denotes the fitness level of the most fitted individuals of the ith trial run, and r is the total number of trial runs.

- **Average number of K clusters**
  The average number of K clusters, $K_{average}$, obtained from the trial runs is calculated as

$$K_{average} = \frac{1}{r}\sum_{i=0}^{r} S_i(x) \tag{8.2}$$

  where $S_i(x)$ denotes the size of the most fitted individuals, from the ith trial run. This value reflects how well the algorithms are able to determine the correct number of clusters.

In addition to the mean value, we employ the *median value* because the mean is sensitive to *extreme values* (or outliers). In our case, if the results from some of the trial runs are unusual compared to the results of the rest. In this case the mean will loose its ability to represent typical or most frequent results of the trial runs.

The median is less sensitive to extreme values since it represents the most frequent results of the algorithms. The median is the center value of a sorted list. For a list of n elements, where n is an odd number, the median m is defined as

$$m = \frac{n+1}{2} \qquad\qquad\qquad (8.3)$$

When n is an even number, the median is the average of the two middle numbers. The median of the K clusters obtained from each trial run is calculated by the same approach as applied to the median of the fitness levels. The median values are denoted as Q_{median} and K_{median}.

We may also measure the convergence speed, *i.e.* the average number of generations it takes for the algorithm to terminate. Termination criteria are described in Section 5.5.

8.2.2. Testing the Parameters

The number of trial runs of each algorithm is set to r =50. For both algorithms, the population size is $p = 50$, maximum size of individuals is $K_{max}= 15$ and maximum number of generations is $t_{max}= 100$. In GCA we employ *Variable K crossover*, *Floating-point mutation* and *Proportional Selection* as evolutionary operators. The mutation rate is set to $p_m= 0.1$ and crossover rate to $p_c= 0.8$. The evolutionary operators used in the DECA is *Adapted binomial crossover* and *Random selection*, where the crossover rate is set to $p_c= 0.7$ and the scaling factor $\beta = 0.5$. To evaluate fitness we apply Davies-Bouldin Index for both algorithms.

8.3. DATA SETS

This section describes the features of the data used for the benchmarking tests. The descriptors of the data sets are summarized in Table **8.3.3**.

8.3.1. Hepta Data Set

The *Hepta* data set is a part of the *Fundamental Clustering Problem Suite (FCPS)*

[37], a set of different clustering problems created for benchmarking purposes. The data set consists of seven well-defined clusters in a three dimensional space. The number of data objects *n* is 212. Since the data set represents a simple clustering problem, we should expect good results for both algorithms. Fig. (**8.1**) shows the optimal clustering structure of the data set in a 3D scatter plot. The image was obtained from the FCPS.

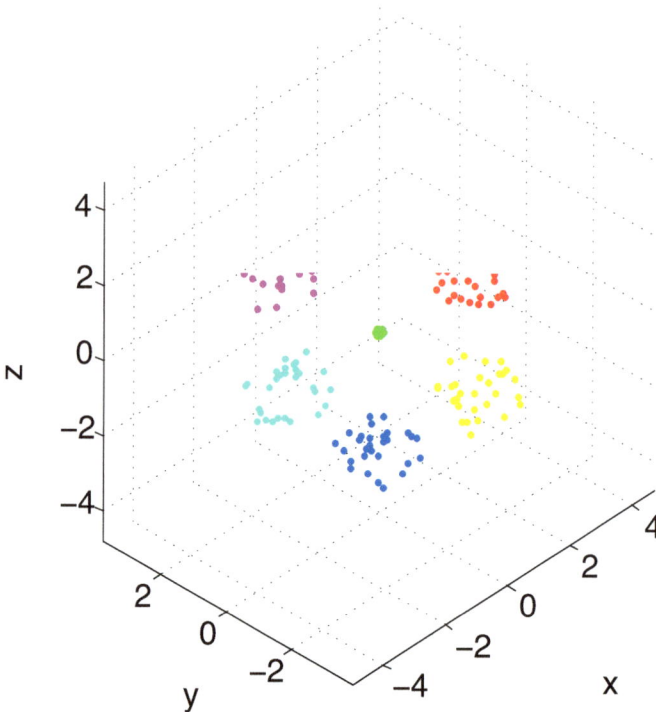

Fig. (8.1). Three-dimensional scatter plot of the *Hepta* data set.

8.3.2. Iris Data Set

The *Iris* data set consists of four measurements of three different species of the Iris flower, collected by Edgar Anderson in 1929 [38] and first applied in 1936 by Sir Ronald A. Fisher [39], as an example of discriminate analysis. The data set is one of the most commonly applied data sets for benchmarking purposes of clustering algorithms. The four measurements describe the *petal* length and width, and the *sepal* length and width, all measured in centimetres. The data set contains three clusters, where one of the clusters is well-separated from the other two. The other two have overlapping points. The data set is available at the *Machine Learning Repository of UCI* [40].

8.3.3. Wine Data Set

The *Wine* data set presents the result from a chemical analysis of three different types of wine, all from the same region in Italy, but from three different cultivars. Each data object consists of 13 attributes describing different features of the wine. Alcohol levels, ash, color intensity and malic acid are some of the features measured. The data set is also available at the *Machine Learning Repository of UCI* [40]. The attributes of the different data sets are given by:

Data set	# of data objects(n)	# of dimensions(d)	actual # of clusters(K)
Hepta	212	3	7
Iris	150	4	3
Wine	178	13	3

8.4. EXPERIMENTS

8.4.1. Hepta

As presumed, both algorithms are able to classify the correct number of clusters K, where both the *GCA* and the *DECA* provide candidate solutions near the optimal number of $K = 7$. The K_{median} is not available, due to some calculation problems. The $Q_{average}$ and Q_{median} of GCA shows that the algorithm provides solutions with a consistent fitness level of each trial run. For DECA, the $Q_{average}$ is a bit lower than Q_{median}, which implies that half of trial runs provides a solution with a fitness level lower than $Q_{median} = 0.6861$. From this we may conclude that in terms of fitness, the GCA performed better than DECA. Both algorithms have a high convergence speed. The GCA on average locates the most fitted individual after 15.34 generations and the DECA after 13.48 generations. Each algorithm terminates if no better solution is found on ten consecutive generations. The results are summarized in Table **8.1**. Fig. (**8.2**) shows a trial run of the GCA. The figure shows that the algorithm is able to classify seven well separated clusters. The clustering structure is compared to the actual clustering structure presented in Fig. (**8.1**).

Table 8.1. Benchmarking results — Hepta data set.

Dataset	Algorithm	Measurements (*DBI*)						
		Generations (mean)	$K_{average}$	K_{median}	$Q_{average}$	Q_{median}	**Best fitness**	**Worst fitness**
Hepta	GCA	15.34	7.08	-	0.6897	0.6861	0.7841	0.3772
	DECA	13.48	6.98	-	0.5409	0.6861	0.7841	0.2529

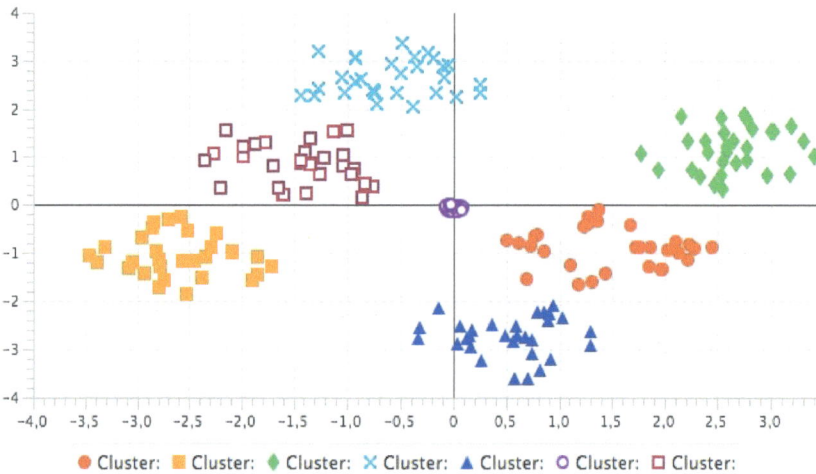

Fig. (8.2). Experiment - a trial run of GCA using the *Hepta* data set.

8.4.2. Iris

Table **8.2** summarizes the results of the experiments on the Iris data set. Both algorithms are consistently providing an optimal value of $K = 2$, where the DECA is a bit more consistent since the $K_{average}$ is closer to the K_{median} than the GCA. In terms of fitness, both algorithms converge to approximately the same value of $Q_{average}$, but the DECA is bit more stable (reflected in a 0.0001 difference between $Q_{average}$ and Q_{median}).

Table 8.2. Benchmarking results — Iris data set.

Dataset	Algorithm	Measurements (*DBI*)						
		Generations (mean)	$K_{average}$	K_{median}	$Q_{average}$	Q_{median}	**Best fitness**	**Worst fitness**
Iris	GCA	15.06	4.7	2.0	0.2337	0.2256	0.3384	0.1856
	DECA	12.06	3.16	2.0	0.2255	0.2256	0.2572	0.1665

From Section 8.3.2, the actual number of clusters in the Iris data set is three, but both the GCA and the DECA are only able to classify two. Fig. (**8.3**) presents a trial run of DECA, where the optimal clustering structure obtained was $K = 2$. The figure shows that there are two well-separated clusters in the data, which means that the third cluster must be inside one of the two clusters, classified by the algorithm. As described in Section 2.1.6, the DBI validates clustering structures based on the measurements of how compact and well-separated the clusters are. From Section 8.3.2, two of the clusters in the Iris data set have points that overlap. Because of the overlapping points, the DBI will provide a better validation result when the two cluster are classified as one cluster, instead of two separate clusters. This reveals a limitation of using the DBI as a fitness measure when optimizing clustering structures, also presented in [3].

▲ Cluster: O Cluster:

Fig. (8.3). Experiment - a trial run of DECA using the *Iris* data set.

8.4.3. Wine

The performance of both algorithms are unsatisfactory in terms of finding the correct number of clusters. The actual number of clusters are three, but the algorithms are converging to a much higher value of K. Even though DECA provides a much lower number of clusters ($K_{average} = 17.28$), than GCA ($K_{average} =$

25.74), neither of them come close to the optimal value of $K = 3$. Fig. (**8.4**) shows the results from a trial run of the GCA. Note that because the number of clusters is higher than eight, different clusters have been assigned the same labels (this limitation of javaFX Scatter Chart class is discussed in chapter 7).

Table 8.3. Benchmarking results — Wine data set.

Dataset	Algorithm	Measurements (*DBI*)						
		Generations (mean)	$K_{average}$	K_{median}	$Q_{average}$	Q_{median}	Best fitness	Worst fitness
Wine	GCA	15.28	25.74	26.0	0.1528	0.1510	0.2394	0.1045
	DECA	27.7	17.28	18.5	0.1824	0.1817	0.2612	0.1328

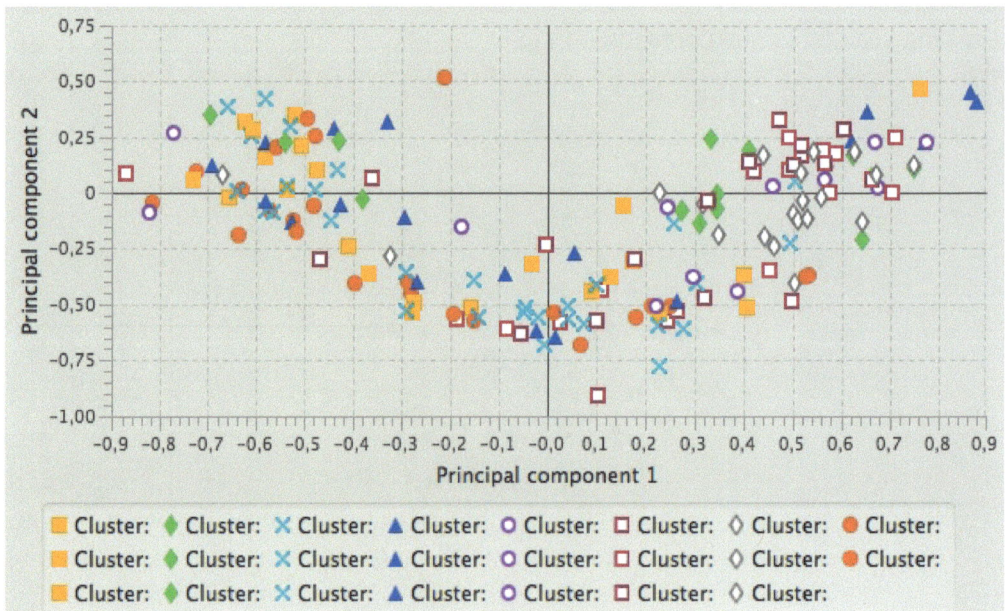

Fig. (8.4). Experiment - a trial run of GCA using the *Wine* data set.

CONCLUSION

Both algorithms performs well in terms of classifying well-defined clusters. However, when presented to data with overlapping clusters none of the algorithms are able to classify the correct number of clusters. As the experiments of the iris data set show, clusters that overlap may be assigned a better DBI value, when classified as one cluster.

This reveals the limitation of the Davies-Bouldin Index as a fitness measure. Ten different runs of a standard K-means algorithm, using the Iris data set, were presented in [41]. The result from each run is validated using the Davies-Bouldin Index. With $K = 2$, the algorithm provides a result of $DBI = 0.687$. In terms of fitness, defined in 5.5.6, this would be evaluated as

$$\frac{1}{DBI} = \frac{1}{0.687} = 1.456 \tag{8.4}$$

When the best solution found by both the GCA and the DECA (see Table **8.2**), is compared to the standard K-Means algorithm presented in [41], we see that the last one gives the best result. This reveals that even if both algorithms are able to provide good solutions in terms of classifying the correct number of clusters, they are not able to exploit the domain K. This will be further discussed in chapter 9.

CHAPTER 9

Discussion

Abstract: In this chapter we discuss different challenges of using evolutionary algorithms to optimize the K-means algorithm. One problem is how to handle empty clusters. In addition, the time complexity of the different algorithms is shown.

Keywords: Convergence speed, Data representation, Empty clusters, Fitness measure, Invalid cluster structures, Time complexity.

9.1. INTRODUCTION

In this chapter, we want to discuss some of the design challenges that we have faced during the process of using evolutionary algorithms to optimize the K-means algorithm.

9.2. DATA REPRESENTATION

The data representation scheme described in Section 5.4, introduces new constraints that we need to handle. When a standard data representation scheme of evolutionary algorithm is used, genes of individuals represent a *finite* set distinct features of the data. This implies that individuals may contain equal values in its genetic material since each value represents a measurement of different dimension. When optimizing clustering structures, duplicates of the genetic material implies invalid clustering structures.

For instane, when an individual x_1, representing a clustering structure K = 3, is initialized with the genetic material

$$x_1 = \{c_1, c_1, c_1\} \tag{9.1}$$

where c_1 is some arbitrary centroid. We see that all three clusters are assigned the same cluster centroid. As a result, when clustering the data (Algorithm **5.4.1**) all data objects will be assigned to the first cluster, leaving the other two clusters empty. This results in an invalid clustering structure. Invalid clustering structures result in incorrect fitness evaluation and must be avoided. Invalid clustering structures are further discussed in Section 9.3.

During the initialization process we want to create a population of distinct individuals to avoid individuals that explore the same parts of the search space. The data representation scheme is described in Section 3.1. When two individuals of size n are compared, we only need to verify that none of the n gene-pairs are equal. This has a time-complexity of $O(n)$. Thus initializing a population of p distinct individuals has the time-complexity of $O(p^2 \cdot n)$. When the representation scheme described in Section 5.4 is used, the initialization of a population becomes a bit more complicated. For instance, two individuals x_1 and x_2, where both represent the clustering structure of $K = 2$, are initialized with the following genetic material

$$x_1 = \{c_1, c_2\}$$

$$x_2 = \{c_2, c_1\}$$

(9.2)

where c_1 and c_2 represent some arbitrary centroids. Since each gene represents a cluster centroid, the relative ordering of the genetic material is trivial. As a result, x_1 and x_2 represent the same clustering structure. To check that two individuals of size n are equal we have to cross-check their genetic material, which has the time-complexity of $O(n^2)$. For a population of size p this results in a time-complexity of $O(p^2 \cdot n^2)$. Some redundancy may be allowed in the initial population, but a population that solely consists of equal individuals will impair the exploration abilities of the algorithm. On the other hand, large data sets reduce the probability of producing redundant individuals. By doing redundancy check we are adding unnecessary computational complexity.

9.3. INVALID CLUSTERING STRUCTURES

To initialize the centroids of K clusters by randomly generating data objects within the boundaries of the search space, one could end up with cluster centroids that are far away from the data undergoing clustering. By this scenario, some of the clusters could end up without members, thus failing to satisfy one of the requirements of partitional clustering, that all clusters have to be non-empty. In a standard K-means algorithm the limitation is handled by randomly selecting data objects from the data set to serve as cluster centroids [42]. Since centroids are sampled from the data set, each cluster will at least have one member. The same approach is used during the initialization process of the ECA, where the genetic material of individuals is randomly sampled from the data set. This ensures that all clustering structures are valid. When evolving the population, the genetic material of the individuals is altered. As a result, it is no longer guaranteed that the clustering structures of the individuals consist of entirely non-empty clusters.

The fitness evaluation of the individuals will be compromised if we allow individuals to represent invalid clustering structures. For instance, the Davies-Bouldin Index of a clustering structure that contains empty clusters is *undefined*, because the intra- and inter-cluster distances of empty clusters cannot be computed. The same situation occurs when we use the clustering metric as a fitness measure. This illustrates that it is necessary to add mechanisms to handle empty clusters of clustering structures, before we evaluate how good they are. Various methods for handling empty clusters in a standard K-means algorithm are described in [42]:

- *Removing empty clusters:* if a cluster is empty after performing clustering, we remove the relevant cluster from the clustering structure.
- *Reinitialize cluster centroids:* if a cluster is empty after performing clustering, one reinitialize the cluster centroid by randomly selecting a data object from one of the other clusters.

With respect to the exploration of the search space, the consequence of *removing* empty clusters, one biases the exploration abilities of the algorithm towards smaller individuals. When we remove empty clusters, we reduce the number of clusters, K, that the individual represents. By *reinitializing* the cluster centroids of empty clusters, we avoid reducing the number of dimensions in the search space. One could end up splitting compact clusters, resulting in a less favourable clustering structure. But this will also yield a lower fitness level, so these individuals will not be favoured during evolution of the population. Fig. (**9.1**) illustrates a two-dimensional scatter plot containing data objects and three cluster centroids ($K=3$). The grey points represent the data objects undergoing clustering, and the red points represent the cluster centroids of three clusters. Due to the positioning of centroid $c3$ in Fig. (**9.1a**), no members will be added to this cluster because centroid $c1$ and $c2$ are closer for all data objects. By reinitializing $c3$ (illustrated in Fig. **9.1b**), by randomly assigning one of the data objects as the new cluster centroid $c3$, we ensure that all clusters will have at least one member.

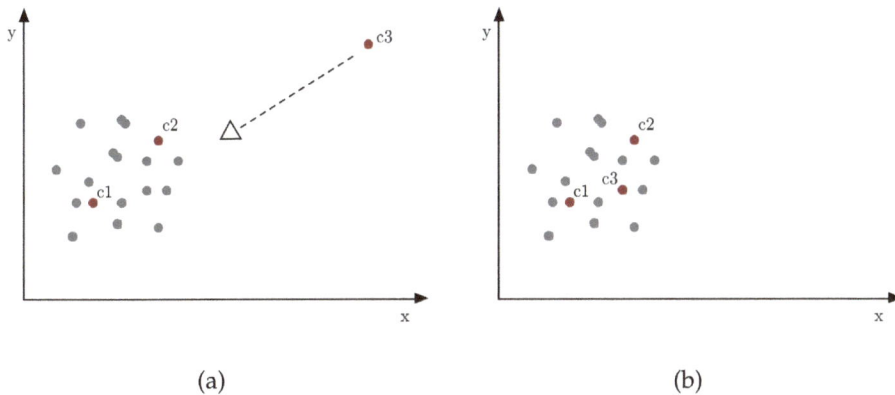

(a)   (b)

Fig. (9.1). Reinitialization of cluster centroids.

By using the principles of evolutionary computation, another approach is to penalize invalid individuals by reducing their fitness level. However, this reduces the probability of being selected for crossover. The problem with this approach is that one subsequently removes good genetic material from the population. Individuals that contain empty clusters could contain good genetic material. However, low fitness level decreases the probability of being selected for the next generation.

We notice that the prior mentioned approach just corrects the invalid clustering structures produced by the evolutionary operators. One should rather prevent the evolutionary operators to create invalid clustering structures. This is achieved by adding a constraint to the evolutionary operators. If the an evolutionary operation results in individuals with invalid clustering structures, the operation should be reversed. This approach is employed in both GCA and DECA. If any of the employed evolutionary operators produces individuals with invalid clustering structures, they will be rejected.

As a result, the individuals selected for an evolutionary operation will remain unchanged. For instance, if the mutation of a gene produces an individual with an invalid clustering structure, this mutation step will be rejected and the gene will not be mutated. A more detailed description on how the constraint is added to the different evolutionary operators is given in Section 5.5. By adding this constraint, evolutionary operators will never produce individuals containing invalid clustering structures. Thus, the evaluation of their fitness level will be correct (using any of the clustering validation methods presented in 2.1.6). This constraint could also increase the time-complexity of both algorithms. To confirm that the alteration of individuals does not result in invalid clustering structures, we have to recluster the data. In addition, this constraint could also result in lower convergence speed, depending on how many evolutionary operations that are rejected. Both the increase in time-complexity and the consequence in terms of the evolution of individuals are discussed in Section 9.5.

9.4. ADAPTING EVOLUTIONARY OPERATORS

How are mutation and crossover operation being performed when evolving clustering structures? This is an essential question when performing crossover. In this case one interchanges the genetic material of individuals to create new off-springs. Usually, the chromosome of individuals consists of genes that represent one value. In Section 5.4, each gene is a data object which means that each gene contains more than one value (depending on the number of dimensions of the data). This means that there exist two ways of interchanging genetic material during crossover:

1. Interchange of cluster centroid values between individuals.
2. Interchange cluster centroids between individuals.

The purpose of a crossover operator is to *exploit* parts of the search space that yields a high fitness level of the individuals. This is done by selecting parents with a high fitness level to create an offspring. Applying the first option could alter the cluster centroids away from their current position in the search space, *i.e.* possibly moving them away form good areas of the search space. The example below shows the result of a crossover operation using the first option. x_1 and x_2 denote the individuals before crossover, and x'_1 and x'_2 denotes the offsprings ($\implies$ illustrates the change of genes between x_1 and x_2).

$$x_1 = \{(10.0, 11.0)\} \implies x'_1 = \{(10.0, 2.0)\}$$
$$x_2 = \{(40.0, 2.0)\} \implies x'_2 = \{(40.0, 11.0)\}.$$

The offsprings contain cluster centroids that are relatively far away from their parents, and thus defeating the purpose of the crossover operator. By using such an approach the properties resemble a mutation operator, where its purpose is to explore the search space by altering the genetic material of the individuals. The second option does not alter the clustering centroids of the parents. It only creates a new combination, to adapt the exploitation requirements to the crossover operator.

9.5. HANDLING INVALID INDIVIDUALS

In Section 9.3 we discussed invalid clustering structures and how these could be handled. In our system we have implemented constraints within the evolutionary operators that prevents the creation of invalid clustering structures. However, adding these constraints has the consequences to increase the time-complexity of both algorithms, and this also will reduce the convergence speed.

9.5.1. Time-Complexity

From Section 5.5, the time-complexity of the two evolutionary clustering algorithms, with the constraints is:

- **Genetic Clustering Algorithm (GCA)**: $O(t \cdot p \cdot n^3 \cdot d)$
- **DE based Clustering Algorithm (DECA)**: $O(t \cdot p \cdot n^2 \cdot d)$

In terms of handling the constraint in the GCA, we need to verify that neither of the evolutionary operators, *i.e.* the *Variable K crossover* operator and the *Floating-point mutation* operator, produce individuals with invalid clustering structures. Without the validity check, these two operations have time-complexities of $O(p \cdot n)$ and $O(p \cdot n \cdot d)$, respectively. The validity check of these two operation results in an increase of the time-complexity of $O(p \cdot n^2 \cdot d)$ and $O(p \cdot n^3 \cdot d)$.

Before the validity check is added, the heaviest operation of GCA is the fitness evaluation with time-complexity of $O(p \cdot n^2 \cdot d)$. This validity check makes the mutation operator the most heavy. This results in an increase in **total time-complexity** from $O(t \cdot p \cdot n^2 \cdot d)$ to $O(t \cdot p \cdot n^3 \cdot d)$.

In terms of the DECA, the validity check increases the time-complexity of these operations:

• *Create trial vector*: $O(p \cdot k \cdot d)$ to $O(p \cdot n^2 \cdot d)$.
• *Adapted Binomial crossover*: $O(p \cdot k^2)$ to $O(p \cdot n^2 \cdot d)$.

According to the total time-complexity of DECA, the constraint only result in an increase by a constant., since the time-complexity of calculating the fitness already has the time-complexity of $O(p \cdot n^2 \cdot d)$. As a result the **total-time complexity** of DECA is not affected by handling this constraint. For the GCA, an increase in the time-complexity of a factor n is quite substantial.

9.5.2. Convergence Speed

The constraints could result in a lower convergence speed. We define the convergence speed as the time it takes for the population to consist of only equal individuals. In order to evolve the population by GCA, we first apply the crossover operator. If this operator produces an offspring with its genetic material representing invalid clustering structures, the offspring will be rejected. Thus, the parents takes its place in the population. After performing crossover, all individuals will be selected for mutation, but only the mutation steps that produce individuals with valid clustering structures are accepted. As a result, the evolution of the population is not only determined by the crossover rate p_c and the mutation rate p_m, but also the probability of either operator to produce invalid individuals. In DECA, the offsprings must have a larger fitness level than its parents, and also represent a valid clustering structure to survive to the next generation. However, the constraint may result in a lower convergence rate for both algorithms, since there is less probability that the population will then evolve.

9.6. FITNESS MEASURE

A standard validation method when evaluating the clustering structure produced by a K-means algorithm is the clustering metric J, defined in Equation 2.11. Such a method evaluates clustering structures based on how compact the clusters are. More compact clusters will then result in a smaller value determined by Equation 2.11, and thus a higher fitness level defined by Equation 5.4. The clustering metric measures intra-cluster distances without reflecting upon inter-cluster distances. As K increases, clusters contain fewer members, *i.e.* the clusters become less compact. Since the clustering metric only measure compactness, an increase in K results in a decrease in J, and as a result, the fitness of the individuals increases. By using the clustering metric as a measure of fitness, the optimal clustering structure is when $K = n$, where n is the number of data objects undergoing clustering. Therefore, J is not suitable as a measure of fitness to compute the optimal number of clusters.

As described in Section 2.1.6, the Davies-Bouldin Index (DBI), in addition to intra-cluster distances also emphasize inter-cluster distances when evaluating clustering structures. This means that an increase in K will not automatically produce an increase in fitness level because the distance between clusters becomes smaller. In terms of DBI, smaller distances between clusters represent worse clustering structures. This implies that the use of DBI as a measure of fitness when optimizing clustering structures is better, compared to the clustering metric J. However, as the experiments in Section 8.4 revealed, we know the DBI has its limitations.

CHAPTER 10

Summary and Future Directions

Abstract: In this chapter we make a summary of how to optimize the K-means clustering algorithm based on evolutionary computing. The system is still missing a user interface to handle invalid user input. Parallel coordinates that may be used as a tool to visualize data in high-dimensional spaces is only given a short introduction. In addition, Particle Swarm Optimization (PSO) is also mentioned to find global solutions to optimization problems.

Keywords: Clustering metric, Invalid cluster structures, Overplotting, Parallel coordinates, PSO.

10.1. SUMMARY

The main goal of this book is to explore the possibilities of adapting an evolutionary algorithm to optimize the K-means clustering algorithm. As a part of our research we wanted to create two evolutionary clustering algorithms, each one using a different paradigm of evolutionary algorithms, and compare their performance. Since there is much research on adapting genetic algorithms to optimize the K-means algorithm, we also want to test out another paradigm of evolutionary algorithm, known as Differential Evolution. Differential Evolution represents a paradigm of evolutionary algorithms that utilizes information about the search space in order to perform a more intelligent search. To compare the performance of the two algorithms, some benchmark tests using data with different characteristics have been done.

A system has been developed where the user may upload data and perform cluster analysis using the two evolutionary clustering algorithms. In addition, two evolutionary operators and fitness evaluation methods have been used, the user may specify the parameters of the algorithms. In order to visualize high-dimensional data in a two-dimensional scatter plot, classical multi-dimensional scaling is used to perform dimension reduction. The data is presenting by two principal components of highest variance. A complete description of the system was given in Chapter 5, with a detailed description of the time-complexity of algorithms used.

The main goal of this book (project), discussed in Chapter 9 is to present different aspects of evolutionary algorithms to optimize the K-means algorithm. This may also result in using different constraints when employing an evolutionary algorithm to optimize the K-means algorithm. The possibility of producing individuals that represent invalid clustering structures implies that all evolutionary operators must contain a constraint that inhibits them from creating invalid individuals. This results in increase of the time-complexity of the GCA, but does not affect the time-complexity of the DECA. We also discussed possible effects the constraints have on the convergence rate.

A case study revealed that both algorithms perform well on data that contain clearly defined clusters. However, both algorithms are struggling with data containing messy clustering structures, due to the limitation of using the Davies-Bouldin Index as a fitness measure. In addition, even though the algorithms are able to find good values of K, the quality level of the solutions was quite low compared to solutions provided by a standard K-means algorithm. This indicates that both algorithms have problems with exploiting the search space to find optimal positions for the cluster centroids.

10.2. ALGORITHM IMPROVEMENTS

10.2.1. Exploitation Abilities

As described in Section 3.1 the purpose of the crossover operator is to *exploit* promising parts of the search space, while the mutation operator should move individuals in different directions with the purpose of *exploring* all parts of the search space. The GCA uses the Variable K crossover operator to explore different values of K, while the Floating-point mutation operator is used to find good positions for the K cluster centroids. One may argue that the behaviour of the two operators does not comply with the behaviour described in Section 3.1, because the Variable K crossover operator explores the search space while the Floating-point mutation operator exploits the space of K. A possible approach is to make the mutation operator to explore the space of K, while the crossover operator is used to exploits the space of the K, with the purpose of locating the optimal position of the K cluster centroids. This may be accomplished by adjusting the crossover operator to produce offspring of equal size of the most fitted parent, while creating a mutation operator that alters the size of the individual.

10.2.2. Invalid Clustering Structures

In Chapter 9 we discussed how empty clusters resulted in incorrect fitness evaluation of individuals. *Reinitialization* of cluster centroids of empty clusters during the fitness evaluation is proposed as a possible solution, but was discarded because one should rather prevent invalid clustering structures being created by the evolutionary operators. We also discussed the possibility that the prevention of invalid clustering structures may lead to a smaller convergence rate since a lot of crossover and mutation operations may be rejected. Rather than rejecting invalid individuals, we may apply the reinitialization approach presented in the discussion, to correct invalid individuals produced by the operators. Rejected individuals may contain good genetic material which is lost when these individuals are rejected.

10.3. SYSTEM IMPROVEMENTS

10.3.1. Error Dialog Boxes

A future improvement is to add functionality that handles invalid input of the user interface. If the user provides a string to the mutation rate instead of a number, the system will crash when the analysis is done. The system should rather display error dialog boxes so the user could provide correct input.

10.3.2. System Output

The system presents the result of the cluster analysis during run-time, both through visualization of the resulting clustering structure and through more specific information, printed to the console. A future improvement is adding functionality so that the results of the analysis is written to a file and stored in the file-system.

10.4. FUTURE WORK

10.4.1. Parallel Coordinates

By using dimension reduction to present the results of the cluster analysis, a lot of information is lost. We have used CMDS to present the data by considering only two dimensions producing the largest variance of the data. Data of lower variance is not presented in this visualization regime. Another way to represent high-dimensional data is using a non-projective mapping method, known as *Parallel coordinates* [7], [43]. Data objects in $\mathbb{R}^d$ is mapped to $\mathbb{R}^2$

$$\mathbb{R}^d \rightarrow \mathbb{R}^2. \tag{10.1}$$

without loosing any information about the data. In a two-dimensional coordinate system d parallel vertical lines are given, each one representing a dimension. These are labelled $v_1, v_2, \ldots, v_d$, illustrated in Fig. (10.1). Each vertical line v_j represent the interval of minimal/maximal value of the j-th dimension, where $j = 1, \ldots, d$. A data object $x = \{x_1, x_2, \ldots, x_3\} \in \mathbb{R}^d$ is represented by a polygonal line ℓ where its vertices are at coordinates $(j - 1, x_j)$ for $j = 1, \ldots, d$. The polygonal line ℓ can be described by $d - 1$ linear equations [43]:

$$\ell : \begin{cases} \ell_{1,2} & : x_2 = m_2 x_1 + b_2, \\ \ell_{2,3} & : x_3 = m_3 x_2 + b_3, \\ & \cdots \\ \ell_{i-1,i} & : x_i = m_i x_{i-1} + b_i, \\ & \cdots \\ \ell_{N-1,N} & : x_N = m_N x_{N-1} + b_N, \end{cases} \tag{10.2}$$

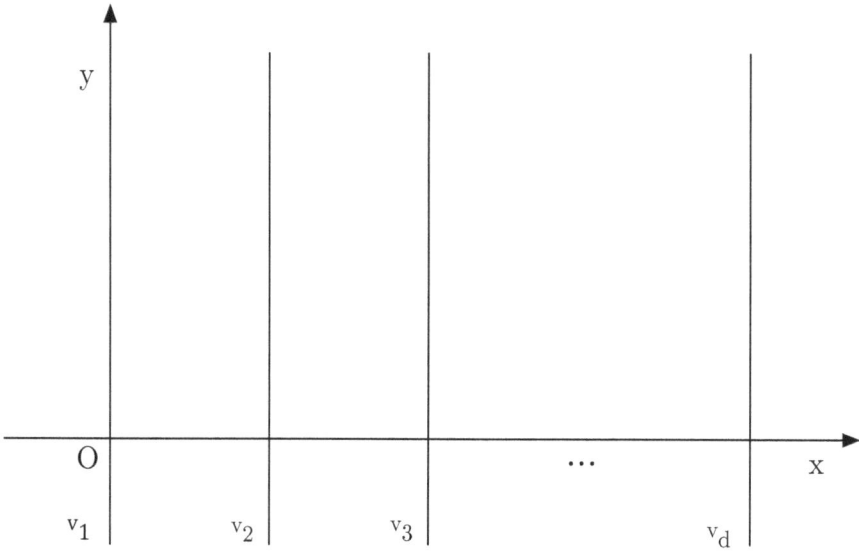

Fig. (10.1). A Parallel Coordinate system.

where m_i denotes the slope of the line $\ell_{i-1,i}$ and b_i denotes intersection with the axes representing x_{i-1}. Fig. (**10.2**) illustrates an example how two points, $x = \{x_1, x_2, x_3, x_4, x_5\}$ and $y = \{y_1, y_2, y_3, y_4, y_5\}$, both $\in \mathbb{R}^5$ are visualized. The purpose of parallel coordinates is to visualize the relationship between the different parameters with the objective of detecting patterns in the data. Parameters can be *positively correlated* [43], meaning that an increase in one will imply an increase in others, and *negatively correlated*, meaning that an increase in one leads to a decrease in others. Relations are most visible between adjacent parameters, making the ordering of axes crucial to recognize interesting relations [44]. For *n* parameters there exist $\frac{n-1}{2}$ different orderings of the axes to cover all adjacencies, see [45]. A meaningful ordering of the axes is a matter of individual evaluation, thus reordering should be an interactive process where the users reorders axes to their personal preference.

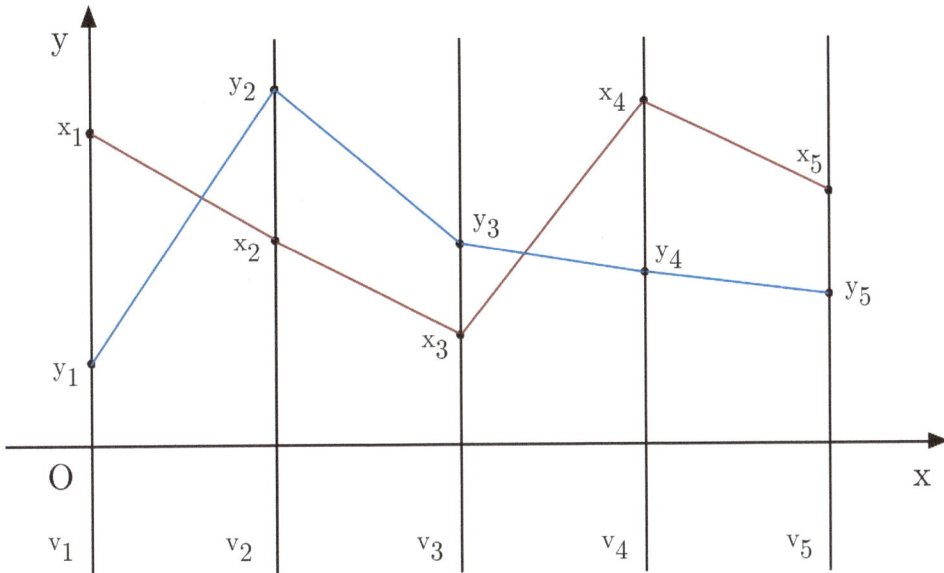

Fig. (10.2). Visualization of two data objects x and $y \in \mathbb{R}^5$.

Parallel coordinates works well when working with data sets consisting of a few hundred data objects. For larger data sets its limitations become evident where the visualization will suffer from *overplotting* [44], illustrated in Fig. (**10.3**). This can be handled by introducing α-blending, a technique where each line is plotted with a $(1-\alpha)$ transparency resulting in a plot where areas with a high density of lines will become more prominent. Thus, it is making parallel coordinates plots more readable. α (where $0 \leq \alpha \leq 1$), represents how transparent an object is, *i.e.* how much of the background is visible through the object. $\alpha = 0$ implies a fully transparent object, while $\alpha = 1$ means that the object is not transparent at all. Fig. (**10.4**) illustrates the visualization of the same data as in Fig. (**10.3**), but with $\alpha = 0.05$. Relations in the data set then becomes more visible. By reordering of the axes, an optimal value of α should be the result of an interactive process where the experiments with different values of α are used to fit the structure of the data.

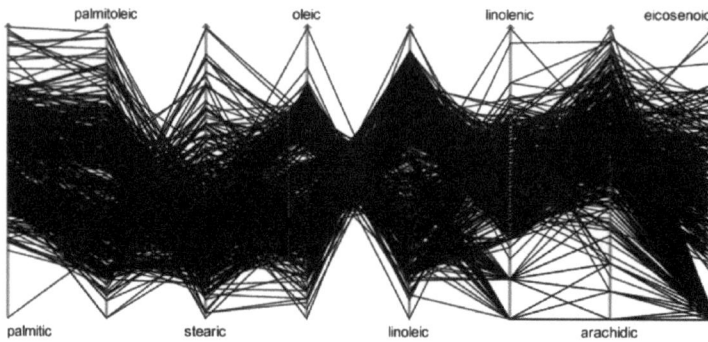

Fig. (10.3). Overplotting.

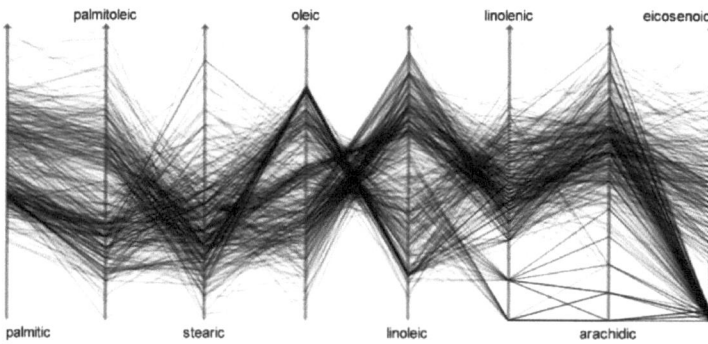

Fig. (10.4). α-blending

10.4.2. Particle Swarm Optimization (PSO)

Particle Swarm Optimization (PSO) is a set of population based search algorithms that simulate the behaviour of bird flocks. PSO has gained a lot of interest because of its efficiency in finding the true global optimal solution of some optimization problems. PSO and Evolutionary algorithms (EA) are both population based heuristic algorithms that search for an optimal solution by altering their population. However, while EA employs evolutionary operators to move its population around in the search space, the individuals of PSO will not alter their position based on their own experiences, but the experiences of their neighbouring individuals. Many experiments have been conducted to compare the two approaches. However, the results of the comparison are highly dependent on the problem domain. In a future study, one aims to adapt the PSO to the K-Means algorithm. The goal is to compare this approach to the evolutionary clustering algorithms presented in the book.

10.4.3. Clustering Validity Indices

Using the *Clustering Metric* and the *Davies-Bouldin Index* the fitness measure of individuals has its drabacks. More research is needed to develop clustering validity indices that are more suitable as fitness measures. A comparison between different indices of fitness of a genetic clustering algorithm, has shown that using the so-called *I*-index, is better to use. It is able to classify the correct number of clusters for nearly any data set [46].

Bibliography

[1]   MailChimp, *How spam filters think,* 2013. Available at: http://kb.mailchimp.com/article/ how-spa-
        -filters-think accessed: 06/09/2013

[2]   D. Cook, D. Swayne, and A. Buja, *Interactive and Dynamic Graphics for Data Analysis: With R and
        GGobi, ser. Use R!.* Springer, 2007, pp. 63-64. [Online] Available at:
        http://books.google.no/books?id=sC0Ij2r_KLcC
        [http://dx.doi.org/10.1007/978-0-387-71762-3_4]

[3]   S. Bandyopadhyay, and S. Pal, "Classification and Learning Using Genetic Algorithms: Applications
        in Bioinformatics and Web Intelligence", In: *ser. Natural Computing Series.* Springer: Berlin
        Heidelberg, 2007. [Online] Available at: http://books.google.no/books?id=jHMGohuVHhgC

[4]   M. Seeger, "Learning with labeled and unlabeled data", In: *Tech. Rep.* University of Ed-Inburgh, 2002.

[5]   Natural History Museum, *What is taxonomy?,* 2013. Available at: http://www.nhm.ac. uk/nature-
        online/science-of-natural-history/taxonomy-systematics/   what-is-taxonomy/index.html accessed:
        23/09/2013

[6]   R. Xu, and D. Wunsch, "Clustering", *IEEE Press Series on Computational Intelligence. Wiley,* 2008.
        [Online]. Available at: http://www.google.no/ books?id=kYC3YCyl_tkC

[7]   G. Gan, C. Ma, and J. Wu, *Data clustering: theory, algorithms, and applications.,* vol. 20. Siam, 2007.
        [http://dx.doi.org/10.1137/1.9780898718348]

[8]   N. K. Visalakshi, and K. Thangavel, "Impact of normalization in distributed K-means clustering", *Int.
        J. Soft Computing,* vol. 4, 2009.

[9]   J.V. Oliveira, and W. Pedrycz, *Advances in Fuzzy Clustering and Its Applications..* John Wiley &
        Sons, Inc.: New York, NY, USA, 2007.
        [http://dx.doi.org/10.1002/9780470061190]

[10]   J.C. Bezdek, *Pattern Recognition with Fuzzy Objective Function Algorithms..* Kluwer Academic
        Publishers: Norwell, MA, USA, 1981.
        [http://dx.doi.org/10.1007/978-1-4757-0450-1]

[11]   D.L. Davies, and D.W. Bouldin, "A cluster separation measure", *IEEE Trans. Pattern Anal. Mach.
        Intell.,* vol. PAMI-1, no. 2, pp. 224-227, 1979.
        [http://dx.doi.org/10.1109/TPAMI.1979.4766909] [PMID: 21868852]

[12]   N. Bolshakova, and F. Azuaje, "Cluster validation techniques for genome expression data", *Signal
        Process.,* vol. 83, no. 4, pp. 825-833, 2003.
        [http://dx.doi.org/10.1016/S0165-1684(02)00475-9]

[13]   A. Engelbrecht, *Computational Intelligence: An Introduction.* 2nd ed Wiley, 2007. [Online]. Available
        at: http://books.google.no/books?id=IZosIcgJMjUC
        [http://dx.doi.org/10.1002/9780470512517]

[14]   D. Simon, *Evolutionary Optimization Algorithms..* Wiley, 2013. [Online]. Available at:
        http://books.google.no/books?id=gwUwIEPqk30C

[15]   R. Adams, and C. Essex, *Calculus: A Complete Course.*. 7th ed Pearson Canada, 2010.

[16]   Z. Michalewicz, "Genetic Algorithms + Data Structures = Evolution Programs", In: *ser. Artificial intelligence.* Springer, 1996. [Online]. Available at: http://books.google.no/books?id=vlhLAobsK68C

[17]   K.P. Wang, and J. Yuryevich, "Evolutionary-programming-based algorithm for environmentally-constrained economic dispatch", In: *Power Systems.,* vol. 13. IEEE Transactions on, 1998.

[18]   I. Sommerville, "Software Engineering", In: *International computer science series.* 8th ed Addison-Wesley, 2007. [Online]. Available at: http://books. google.no/books?id=B7idKfL0H64C

[19]   S. Dasgupta, C. Papadimitriou, and U. Vazirani, *Algorithms,* McGraw-Hill Education, 2008. [Online]. Available at: http://books.google.no/books?id=LaIqnwEACAAJ

[20]   R. Martin, "Agile Software Development: Principles, Patterns, and Practices", *ser. Alan Apt Series,* Prentice   Hall/Pearson   Education,   2003.   [Online].   Available:http://books.google.no/ books?id=0HYhAQAAIAAJ

[21]   Oracle, "What is javafx", Available at: http://docs.oracle.com/javafx/2/overview/ jfxpub-overview.htm accessed: 06/03/2014.

[22]   The Apache Software Foundation, *Apache maven project,* 2014. Available at: http:// maven.apache. org/accessed: 07/01/2014.

[23]   Git, *About,* 2014. Available at: http://git-scm.com/about/ accessed: 07/01/2014.

[24]   GitHub, Inc., *Github,* 2014. Available at: https://github.com/accessed: 07/01/2014.

[25]   D.S. Kent Beck, "Erich Gamma and M. Clark", *Junit,* 2012. Available at: http://junit.org/accessed: 07/11/2013.

[26]   U. Maulik, and S. Bandyopadhyay, "Genetic algorithm-based clustering technique", *Pattern Recognit.,* vol. 33, no. 9, pp. 1455-1465, 2000.
[http://dx.doi.org/10.1016/S0031-3203(99)00137-5]

[27]   H. Yuan, and J. He, "Evolutionary design of operational amplifier using variable-length differential evolution algorithm", *Computer Application and System Modeling (ICCASM)* International Conference, vol. 4, pp. V4-610-614, 2010.

[28]   A. Telea, "Data Visualization: Principles and Practice", In: *ser. Ak Peters Series.* A K PETERS Limited (MA), 2008. [Online]. Available: http://books.google.no/books?id=OFEmGQAACAAJ

[29]   T. Munzer, "Visualization", In: *Fundamentals of Computer Graphics, ser. Ak Peters Series..* Taylor & Francis, 2009, pp. 675-712.

[30]   D. Mize, *Compose,* 2014. Available at: http://3.bp.blogspot.com/_vHdM2yoeMlM/ SZsomzDKYlI/ AAAAAAAAD1s/mfuhg6cuARU/s1600/colorwheel_1.jpgaccessed: 08/02/2014

[31]   OrgeBot, *Scale of saturation,* 2014. Available at: http://commons.wikimedia.org/wiki/File:Saturat iondemo.pngaccessed: 09/02/2014

[32]   D.   Shark,   *The   hsl   color   model   mapped   to   a   cylinder.*   Available   at: http://commons.wikimedia.org/wiki/File:HSL_color_solid_cylinder_alpha_ lowgamma.pngthis file is licensed under the Creative Commons Attribution-Share Alike 3.0 Unported license.

[33]   I. Borg, and P. Groenen, *Modern Multidimensional Scaling: Theory and Applications, ser. Springer Series in Statistics,* Springer, 2005. [Online]. Available at: http://www.google.no/books?id=duTODldZzRcC

[34]   Algorithmics Group, *MDSJ: Java library for multidimensional scaling (version 0.2),* 2009. Available at: http://www.uni-marburg.de/fb12/datenbionik/data? language_sync=1

[35]   S. Stober, C. Hentschel, and A. Nurnberger, "Multi-facet exploration of image collections with an adaptive multi-focus zoomable interface", *Neural Networks (IJCNN), The 2010 International Joint Conference on. IEEE,* 2010pp. 1-8
[http://dx.doi.org/10.1109/IJCNN.2010.5596747]

[36]   S. Ramnath, and B. Dathan, "Object-Oriented Analysis and Design", *ser. Undergraduate Topics in Computer Science,* Springer, 2010. [Online] Available at: http://books.google.no/books?id=2oLOia08YZ0C

[37]   A. Ultsch, *Fundamental clustering problem suite,* 2014. Available at: http://www. uni-marburg.de/fb12/datenbionik/data?language_sync=1 Accessed: 05/04/2014

[38]   E. Anderson, "The species problem in iris", *Annals of the Missouri Botanical Garden,* vol. 23, pp. 457-509, 1936. Available: http://biostor.org/reference/11559
[http://dx.doi.org/10.2307/2394164]

[39]   R.A. Fisher, "The use of multiple measurements in taxonomic problems", *Ann. Eugen.,* vol. 7, no. 2, pp. 179-188, 1936.
[http://dx.doi.org/10.1111/j.1469-1809.1936.tb02137.x]

[40]   K. Bache, and M. Lichman, *UCI machine learning repository,* 2013. Available at: http://archive.ics.uci.edu/ml

[41]   S. Saitta, B. Raphael, and I.F. Smith, "A bounded index for cluster validity", In: *Machine Learning and Data Mining in Pattern Recognition..* Springer, 2007, pp. 174-187.
[http://dx.doi.org/10.1007/978-3-540-73499-4_14]

[42]   F. Torrent-Fontbona, V. Muñoz Solà, and B. López Ibáñez, *Solving large location-allocation problems by clustering and simulated annealing.* 2013.

[43]   A. Inselberg, "Parallel Coordinates: Visual Multidimensional Geometry and Its Applications", *ser. Advanced series in agricultural sciences,* Springer, 2009. [Online]. Available at: http://books.google.no/books?id=DkQlVpv6kzsC
[http://dx.doi.org/10.1007/978-0-387-68628-8]

[44]   M. Theus, "High-dimensional data visualization", In: *Handbook of Data Visualization, ser. Springer Handbooks Comp.Statistics.* Springer: Berlin Heidelberg, 2008, pp. 151-178. [Online].
[http://dx.doi.org/10.1007/978-3-540-33037-0_7]

[45]   E.J. Wegman, "Hyperdimensional data analysis using parallel coordinates", *J. Am. Stat. Assoc.,* vol. 85, no. 411, pp. 664-675, 1990.
[http://dx.doi.org/10.1080/01621459.1990.10474926]

[46]   S. Bandyopadhyay, and U. Maulik, "Nonparametric genetic clustering: comparison of validity indices", *Systems, Man, and Cybernetics, Part C: Applications and Reviews, IEEE Transactions on,* vol. 31, no. 1, pp. 120-125, 2001.

SUBJECT INDEX

www.ingramcontent.com/pod-product-compliance
Lightning Source LLC
Chambersburg PA
CBHW041729210326
41598CB00008B/824